ALL HELL NEEDS IS WATER

- Budge Ruffner

This 1999 publication includes the full manuscript of the 1972 edition plus three stories which Budge Ruffner had chosen for the first edition.

In commemoration of a good life well lived, this new edition of his first book is presented to his family, friends, and admirers, and to those who never had the pleasure of knowing him, by his wife and daughter, Elisabeth and Melissa.

PRIMROSE PRESS
P.O. BOX 2577
PRESCOTT, AZ 86302-2577

ISBN 0-9673171-O-X
SAN 299-9331

To the "Ol' Boys" who told me the tales,
to my children who will remember them.
and to Bette
who urged me to put them on paper.

– Budge Ruffner, 1972

To Bonnie

Melissa Ruffner

Elisabeth Ruffner

Foreward

Lester Ward "Budge" Ruffner was born in Prescott, Arizona on March 17, 1918, into a pioneer Arizona family who had arrived in the territory in 1867. His great-uncle, Morris Andrew Ruffner, filed the first copper claims near where Jerome now stands.

His parents were Mary Ethelyn (Ward) Ruffner, the first public school music teacher in the Arizona Territory, and Lester Lee Ruffner. Lester Lee operated the Ruffner Funeral Home, a business which his brother, George, won at the Palace Saloon on Whiskey Row in January of 1903. The wager that night centered around an unpaid livery bill owed by the undertaker, Frank Nevins, to Ruffner's Plaza Stables. In the best tradition of the old west, the business changed hands at the turn of a card - the business continues and is today the only funeral home from territorial days still in operation.

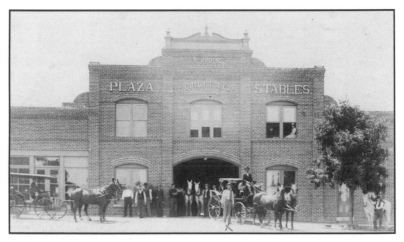

Ruffner Plaza Stables, southeast corner of Goodwin and Montezuma, circa 1900. The "x" at the bottom of the photo marks George Ruffner who was also sheriff of Yavapai County, off and on, beginning in 1894. At the time of his death in 1933, George Ruffner was Arizona's oldest peace officer - both in years of service and age - and the first man from Arizona inducted into the Hall of Great Westerners at the Cowboy Hall of Fame in Oklahoma City. Photograph courtesy of the Ruffner Collection.

Budge was an unremarkable student until he attended Brophy Prep in Phoenix, where strict Jesuit priests taught him to study to remember, read to think, and write to inform, persuade and amuse, according to Don Dedera, writing in his introduction to Ruffner's last book, *Ruff Country: Tales West by Southwest:*

"By Budge's own reckoning, his two most formative, mid-'teen summers were passed as Model A Ford driver and camp ('broken yolk, burnt bacon') cook for expeditions led by Barnard College anthropologist, Gladys Reichard, for field studies in Navajoland in and beyond northeastern Arizona...He also sat by the hour around the evening fire listening to Reichard sermonize against white ethnocentrism, and promote greater appreciation for an Athabaskan tribe that had prevailed - their value system, arts, matriarchal order, religion and language intact - through centuries of foreign invasion and cultural stress.

"'She taught me,' recalled Budge sixty years later, 'to judge people by their standards and not my own.'"

Budge attended Loyola University in Los Angeles and graduated from Cincinnati College of Embalming in 1939. Upon returning to Arizona, he entered the family business. In August of 1940 he married Elisabeth "Bette" Ruffner of Cincinnati, Ohio, and they honeymooned in Arizona's Indian country. Subsequently, Budge enlisted in the Army Air Corps and served until 1943.

A giver to his community and state, Budge organized the 20/30 Club in 1943 to facilitate the continuation of Prescott's Frontier Days celebration and the World's Oldest Rodeo, which his Uncle George had helped to organize in 1888. His father, Lester, served as rodeo chairman and arena director for a number of years. Budge was chairman of Prescott's Centennial Commission and was chosen "Man of the Year" for 1965-66. In 1964, he became a columnist for the Prescott Courier, penning stories of the Southwest which he loved so much. Over the years he wrote articles and reviews for Arizona Highways magazine, New Mexico magazine, Arizona Attorney magazine, Southwest Art, Western Folklorist and *Poems Southwest* and

Arizona Anthem. Budge was also the author of three books, *All Hell Needs Is Water* (1972), *Shot In The Ass With Pesos: A Collection of Frontier Tales* (1979), and *Ruff Country: Tales West by Southwest* (1994). With his daughter, Melissa, he co-authored the *Arizona Territorial Sampler: Food and Lifestyles of a Frontier* (1982, now in its 3rd edition).

The long list of his community and state involvement includes charter member of the Prescott Corral of Westerners in 1962 and acting as its president in 1964. He served two terms as president of the Arizona Historical Society and was recipient of its coveted Al Merito award. Budge was a member of the Indian Commission of the State of Arizona and a member and chairman of the Arizona Lottery Commission, appointed by then Governor Bruce Babbitt. He was a charter member of the Arizona Historical Foundation, at the invitation of his lifetime friend, the late Senator Barry Goldwater. Budge introduced Barry Goldwater on the steps of the Yavapai County Courthouse for every announcement the Senator made for national office (including his presidential bid), save his last senatorial race. Budge also taught as adjunct professor of Southwestern history and literature at both Yavapai College and Prescott College.

Don Dedera wrote of his longtime friend and colleague at Arizona Highways magazine:

"Then what are we to do with this huge, western-dressed *hombre* with a laugh loud enough to fell ponderosa pines? Who lurches through social gatherings, shamelessly bragging about his honored historian wife, Elisabeth, their three children and eight grandchildren, one-of-a-kind cronies, his sassy and sometimes snooty hometown, its surrounding countryside, and the hosts of Indians, Jews, Mexicans, Slavs, Blacks - ministers, murderers, politicians, priests, lawmen, sainted and painted ladies - fools, leaders, connivers, gamblers and achievers - that he met in the flesh or encountered in history?

"What to do with this minstrel who into his eighth decade continues to commit to paper his discoveries and ideas? At least, he is a living treasure of Yavapai County. Probably of Arizona. Possibly of the nation.

"Why...let us ENJOY him!"

Budge wrote in a letter to the University of Arizona Press in 1971:

" My entire life I had listened to what I guess would be folk history - the stories my father and grandfather and all of their friends told each other repeatedly. To me it represented a part of Arizona [and] the southwest which seldom sees ink, and I felt, at least, there was a gap of the past created by this neglect. [This] book is only that. Some of the stories I have either witnessed, participated in, or heard in my life in this State."

And in an undated note, he continued: "Wherever it was, in a comfortable ranch home living room, around a campfire, or in the confined cab of a pick-up truck, the storytelling always ended the same way: one of us would say 'somebody should write that down.' Indeed, somebody should. These little slivers of folklore and history should at least be given the dignity and immortality of print. Our children should know about them, and their children, and their children's children. How much has already gone down the tunnel of time.

"Sometime later an old cowboy friend told me an amusing story. I wrote it down. I love to travel around the Southwest and to be honest about it, I love to talk. It took me quite awhile though, to learn to listen. I traveled, I talked, and I listened, to college professors and cowboys, to bankers and bums, to old-timers and Indians, from San Diego to Amarillo, from the Tetons to Tucson, right here, in one of the most fascinating parts of the world. Then I wrote it down."

Editors' Note:

Budge's last article for Arizona Highways appeared in the July 1996 issue which featured Prescott. He reminisced about sliding down the steel pole at the firehouse; craning his neck as the "Human Fly" scaled the front of a downtown three-story building, alone and unaided; watching movies at the Elks Theater featuring Tom Mix at the Stewart Ranch near Camp Wood or in Granite Dells (Mix once gave him a pony after Budge broke his collarbone trying to emulate one of his movie stunts); or listening as locals recalled visiting with hometown boy, now Mayor of New York City, Fiorello LaGuardia, who had spent six of his growing-up years here when his father was stationed at Fort Whipple during the 1890s.

He concluded with his favorite retort, when he was asked, as he often was, if he had lived here all his life:

"Not yet!" he'd laugh, "but I intend to!"

On May 14, 1996, Budge Ruffner "rode away from the campfire." We like to think he is listening to all the good ol' boys who told him these stories, telling them to him once again.

Photograph courtesy of the Ruffner Collection.

Contents

The Ash Creek Gourmets

Today the vast majority of ranches in Arizona send their cattle to market in huge trucks which take on the animals at the loading chutes of the ranches and in a matter of hours deliver them to their market destinations. This involves a minimum of effort for both cattleman and trucker and the cattle arrive in prime condition to command a top price. Fifty years ago there were no cattle trucks. There were, however, railroads, and ranchers like Charlie Hooker drove their stock to the nearest railhead. The benevolent railroad allowed one cowboy to ride free with every three carloads of animals.

Before World War I, Hooker owned a well-run outfit on Ash Creek which is now Orme School. When marketing time came, Hooker drove his cattle overland the fifteen miles to Mayer and loaded them on the train for Phoenix, where the cattle were delivered to the buyer. The relief of this responsibility, plus the sudden affluence created by the sale, frequently led the boss man to spring for a few drinks for the cowhands and top the celebration with a dinner at the old American Kitchen on Central Avenue in Phoenix.

Charlie Hooker was a generous man, and not the type to flout such a gallant tradition. After the cattle were delivered and the basic social amenities observed, he herded his men to the big oak table in the back room of that fine old Chinese establishment. It was a sacrilege, of course, to order anything but steak, so the bashful, tongue-tied cowboys sat patiently while the boss ordered from the menu, then unanimously agreed that whatever he had ordered was good enough for them. This plan had always worked well for them, but this time, feeling a little adventuresome, the boss ordered with the steak, an artichoke.

A half century ago, artichokes were seldom seen along the banks of Ash Creek. To have such a gastronomical offering placed before him created deep-seated anxieties in a cowboy. Each one waited for another to demonstrate the method of eating this odd bloom. No one ever suspected that Charlie Hooker had yet to consume his first artichoke. Finally, one brave soul broke the tension by liberally sprinkling his with salt and pepper, picking up his knife and fork and cutting it to shreds. Every man at the table methodically repeated the process, then mechanically and indifferently, each man pushed a generous portion of the thorny leaves into his mouth. They hacked and squirmed and coughed, eyes watered and facial muscles twitched. Water offered little relief and chewed beefsteak only served as a temporary padding.

One sufferer allowed as how it must be a midget Spanish bayonet or yucca plant. Another reckoned as how he would just as soon try to eat a pine cone. It was the last time the Ash Creek gang ever charged an artichoke.

Man's Best Friend

The following story is true. Only the dog's name has been changed to protect the innocent. It may make you wonder, is the dog really man's best friend? Surely, he would have many defenders if his traditional role should ever be seriously challenged or questioned. Perhaps today there are too many lovely and long-held beliefs which are being pricked by the pin of new thought. Here is at least one incident when the dog was anything but man's best fried.

Lee Murphy was a typical cowboy, if there is such a thing. He lived in Williamson Valley. He was active on the ranges of northern Arizona in the nineteen twenties and thirties when the man and horse were still the principal and most effective tools of the business of producing cattle. Summer on the working cattle ranch was a busy time, and fall, because of the round-up, was even a more demanding time of year. Long hours were spent in the saddle, and a cowboy had little motivation to waste valuable time grooming or in the pursuit of his personal toilette.

But this was a different kind of day. Lee was through with his most pressing chores, he was alone in the woods, and a clear and very appealing pool formed by a sometime mountain stream tactfully invited him to bathe. Of course, there was no change of clean clothes here but he did have a bar of soap in the saddle bag, and it was a warm, bright day.

Lee swung off his horse and stripped off his clothes, piling them in a heap for his dog to guard. The dog settled near the clothing to sleep as a sentinel and Lee waded into the nearby pool for his frequently postponed bath. McCoy was the dog's name – a constant companion: the usual shepherd of black-white-brown, with at least one "glass eye." He pledged his unending allegiance to whoever fed him occasionally and sometimes stroked his thick, shiny coat.

So unexpectedly enjoyable was this rare combination of fresh air, clean water, soap and warm sun, that several minutes passed before Lee entertained the idea of returning to his clothes the noble dog was guarding. As far as the dog was concerned, the fleshy white apparition that emerged from the creek and approached the pile of clothing was a stranger. He didn't look right. He certainly didn't smell right. McCoy sprang to all fours and assumed the posture of a faithful protector. His hackles bristled, his mouth receded in a toothy snarl. He growled and snapped and barked. A good bath had made Lee a stranger to his closest companion. How long the agonizing process of recovering his clothes took Lee, I do not know. Several attempts were made before he finally convinced the dog of his identity. Certainly, Lee was shaken by the experience, but what I have often wondered about was the dog. He must have had his doubts 'til the day he died.

The Immortal River

In northern Colorado near Poudre Pass, at an elevation of 10,175 feet, the Colorado River is born. A marshy mountain meadow catches the seeps of the surrounding timber slopes and channels them into a tiny crystal stream a few inches wide.

From this point, the river starts to live its 1,400-mile life till it dies in a songless sea between two shores of Mexico. By the time it reaches Lee's Ferry, sixteen miles below Lake Powell, it has matured and become sure of itself. For the next 300 miles it mills, gnaws, and chews at the floor and ancient baseboards of the Grand Canyon.

To run this 300-mile stretch of the river is, I suppose, the dream of almost every Arizonan I have ever known. But the effect it has on one is surprising. It changes your sense of values. The river is a stern teacher that generates instant respect.

The canyon furnishes intimate beauty and grandeur far beyond one's usual expectations. Living in it and traveling through it for eight days is an experience with strange emotional qualities.

Our party consisted of thirty people; five crew members and twenty-five in the group who varied from corporate executives to college students. The youngest was nineteen and the oldest, a native Arizonan, nearly seventy-five-years old, who was forced to crowd all this magnificent scenery through his one remaining eye.

The man who supplied the boats, equipment and know-how was Jerry Sanderson of Page, a second-generation river

17

runner who knows and therefore respects the river. His equipment is superb; he selects his crew with care, but the quality of his party is left to the gods of chance; here again he was lucky.

We had an anthropologist in the group who is the best informed man in the world today on the archaeology of the Grand Canyon; two men from the United States Geological Survey, a geologist and a hydrologist, both well versed on the Canyon; a history professor from the University of Utah in the process of doing his second book on the canyonlands of the Southwest; and literally a raft of other talented people who know how to repair a a pair of glasses with a Band-Aid, identify a strange bird, dry out a bedroll in record time, predict the weather, or compact an empty beer can with their bare hands. (There were several valiant volunteers who emptied them.) We had three young and temporarily single men with us who charged every cliff and chowline at a full gallop and did their share of the work and more.

Undoubtedly the most attractive camp we had was at Deer Creek Falls, which was best described by one of the group as looking like a set from an old Johnny Weismuller movie. It is a clear ribbon waterfall, seventy-five feet high, against a fern-covered sandstone cliff, and it creates a pool where native rainbow trout are plentiful. It was at this camp that we witnessed a once-in-a-lifetime sight. A thunderstorm on the South Rim created a 1,000-foot waterfall, reddish-brown and free-falling till it spewed into a grove of mesquite trees at the base of the cliff. It flowed vigorously for about an hour, then stopped as suddenly as it had begun; but in that hour it created another change in the topography of the Grand Canyon; the water that carved that change had joined the river on its way to the sea.

We saw Indian ruins and historic sights and constantly referred to a cheery little map that listed and dated the various fatalities of each rapid. It was a great morale builder but not until you had run that particular rapid. The lexicon of any river guide worth his salt contains such choice words and phrases as blowout, upset, collapse, shudder, wipeout, rip, submerge, survivors, and whirlpool. Our pilots were masters and sprinkled their commentary with these little stiletto phrases.

It is a trip you should share with friends and family for it is thrilling in every sense of the word. It is honestly primitive and creates the reality of primitive values. It shrinks ego but sharpens respect; it is sort of a watery highway to a whole new world of very old ideas. In this sense the river is life itself, for it still goes on when you are no longer there.

Floating on the Colorado River, 1967. Photograph courtesy of the Ruffner Collection.

Budge Ruffner's first great-grandchild, Christopher Andrew, running the river for the first time at age ten, in April 1995. Photograph courtesy of the Ruffner Collection.

The Final Tribute

Shortly after the turn of the century, the little town of Ash Fork, some fifty miles to the west of Flagstaff, was booming. The railroad had come – indeed had created Ash Fork – and had brought with it many changes for the natives of the area. Cattle had been the staff of life, but now many sheep operations had moved in, and while the conflict between the two never reached the violence that TV and the movies would lead one to believe, much bitterness boiled and festered between the sheep and cattle men.

Elcy Brown was a native. He was a cowboy, and a good one. His entire life had been spent on the cattle ranges of Arizona and the badges of his profession were his proudest possessions. While Elcy's home was in Ash Fork, he worked where there was work to do, and this particular spring he was on a ranch in southern Arizona near Globe.

The mood was a happy one that morning, as it usually is when roundup starts. A good night's sleep and a generous cow-camp breakfast did much to create a feeling of fun and celebration. Elcy was on a strange horse, but this did not stop him from expressing his exuberance by "dabbing" his rope onto a young bull. In the tradition of the Texas-trained cowboy, his rope was tied "hard and fast" to the saddle horn. The bull charged to the end of the rope, catching the horse unawares, causing him to rear and fall over backwards, crushing his rider. That was the way Elcy Brown died, as a cowboy.

His body was brought to Ash Fork. The funeral was to

take place in the community church, a small frame building not unlike a thousand others scattered over the rural areas of America. The services, however, were somewhat unique, for while the funeral was to be held at four in the afternoon, the body was to be viewed in the church by all comers from noon on. This four-hour period served a real purpose as a sort of preparation time, and all of Elcy's old cowboy friends consumed the four hours and three times that amount of whiskey. The time was spent by these mourners walking between the church and the saloon, confirming the reality of Elcy's death by visiting the church and then hurrying to the saloon to blot out the memory of what they had just seen. A young Baptist minister was to conduct the services, but the family had asked Al Smith, a cherished friend, to say a few words at the funeral as a last tribute to Elcy. Al Smith was a cowman, too, and one of the most bitter opponents of the recent invasion by the sheep of the grasslands once the exclusive territory of cattle.

The church was packed and by the time Al was called upon to address the multitude, whatever inhibitions he had harbored concerning public speaking had vanished. The eulogy was magnificent. If not the most scholarly, it was certainly the most sincere tribute to a cowboy ever heard in the environs of Ash Fork. Steadying himself on the podium, Al said:

"Look at him folks; there he lays, a cowboy to the end. Born in a country of open cattle range amid the smell of sweat of horses and cowboys. Raised on the range beneath the sun and stars of the old west, his entire life was that of a cowboy, living among real men, horses and cattle. A friend around a campfire, a man you could count on a-horseback. He died the way a cowboy would be proud to die, a bull on one end of his rope and his saddle horn tied to the other. He wasn't butted to death by no God-damned SHEEP!"

Well Worth It

I guess you would have to call him a pioneer. The dictionary I use defines pioneer as "one who ventures into the unknown." Well, he was one, he did venture, and I doubt very much that he ever knew where he was. He was, then, one who ventured into the unknown – a pioneer.

He was a mean old man. To give you some idea of the magnitude of his malice, a man who knew him told me "he would get on his horse and ride away from you just so he could yell at you." Not a very pretty picture, is it? He settled in southern Yavapai County a century ago with an overly obedient wife and their first-born. In the years that followed he prospered: a ranch, which he created by territorial aggression and neighbors' inattention; a few mining claims which contained some ore and many unfulfilled promises; calico cattle which had been willing victims of a long rope; and a windfall of naive travelers crossing the country. Even today the rumors persist as to where and how their journeys ended.

The old man was, by the most modest standards something less than an ideal husband. By his eight children, seven of whom were born after he arrived in Arizona, he was looked upon as being about as compassionate as Attila the Hun. His wife was well aware that her marriage fell somewhat short of the American dream; the little parental allegiance which existed among his offspring was nurtured by fear rather than love.

When his children were near the end of their ordeal of dependency, the old man sold one of his mining claims to an

Eastern syndicate for twenty thousand dollars. He was well aware that his children desired to leave home, so somewhat out of his traditional character, decided to aid them in this goal. He put six thousand dollars aside as his own and divided the remainder among seven of his eight children, giving them two thousand dollars apiece.

The one son whom he chose to ignore was David. He had never been fond of David. This lack of love had brought the expected bloom of resentment from the young man. The father compounded his cruelty by announcing to the entire family that he had always strongly suspected that David was not of his issue, and therefore had chosen this method to disavow him. Everyone, of course, expected David's anger to erupt but his calm and uncommon reaction concluded the unhappy relationship.

"Hell," he said, "two thousand dollars is a mighty cheap price to pay to find out that I ain't no kin to the mean old son-of-a-bitch."

Old Antoine

Among the fur traders and pathfinders of early Arizona, Antoine Leroux stands as a giant. Born in St. Louis in 1801, he was among the one hundred enterprising young men who in 1822 joined the Ashley-Henry expedition to the headwaters of the Missouri River. He was, however, not the usual type of escapist to the fur trade. Leroux was well educated, the son of a wealthy St. Louis family which was tremendously proud of its French and Spanish blood. His way on the upper Missouri among the rowdy and robust Rocky Mountain fur brigades was brief, and in 1824 he established his headquarters in Taos, New Mexico. Here there was a reasonable market for his beaver plews, as well as a semblance of social life, which appealed to a young man who had been raised in the tradition of the good life.

From Taos, Leroux trapped beaver in southwest Colorado, and his name was given to two streams and a mountain pass in the area. Like most fur traders, he graduated to Scout and Guide, and led four Army expeditions from New Mexico to California, as well as a number of punitive forays with the United States Army against the Indians. This young man was not devoid of business acumen, for he became a Mexican citizen to avoid the taxes imposed on gringos, and married the heiress to a half-million-acre land grant. The first years as a resident of Taos were spend mostly in the field, trapping. He trapped the Gila and Colorado rivers as well as the Bill Williams fork of the Colorado.

Colonel Philip St. George Cooke selected Leroux to guide the Mormon Battalion to San Diego. Antoine's clever field work played a significant part in causing the Mexican Army to withdraw from Tucson. He was commended by Cooke for courage and sobriety at a time in history when the latter was more of a common characteristic in the Army than the former.

Leroux again in 1847 was a valuable aid to Lt. W.H. Emory of the Topographic Engineers; his maps and trails guided thousands of later emigrants to the California gold fields. The expedition of Capt. Lorenzo Sitgreaves in 1851 chose Leroux as a guide on this important survey across northern Arizona. The group met numerous hostile Indians, and Leroux was wounded by three arrows driven into his arm, scalp, and wrist. The ambush occurred a few miles west of the present-day Flagstaff. However, he continued the trip to the river and Yuma before returning to Taos.

Antoine's last important scouting trek was with Lt. A.W. Whipple in 1853-54. The party was delayed by smallpox and forced to make a prolonged camp on the Little Colorado River until the sick had recovered. This survey was later used by the Atlantic and Pacific Railroad when they built their tracks across northern Arizona.

Following the Whipple survey, Leroux lived the remainder of his life at his ranch near Taos, where he died in 1861. His last years were spent as a gentleman farmer and politician of note. Few of Arizona's travelers today are aware of his tremendous contributions, but his name is imprinted on the land.

Desert Tragedy

There is an obscure sliver of Arizona history which has all the drama of the Alamo of Texas, all the shock impact of the Donner Party's trek into California, and all the raw material of the legend of Custer's Last Stand. It is referred to as the Oatman Massacre, for six members of this family were killed by Indians. Had it been the other way around, the watercolor words of history would have probably called it a battle.

Royce and Mary Ann Oatman and their seven children were in Independence, Missouri, in 1850 to join a party of fifty people and eight wagons to journey the well-worn trail to California. Two years earlier the Mexican War had ended, and gold had been found in California. Both of these events triggered an exodus from East to West of optimistic fortune hunters and potential empire builders.

The Oatman family was not a typical emigrant party of the period. While not wealthy, they did have ample funds for the trip and to reestablish themselves upon their arrival in California. Their equipment was above average, but their limited knowledge of the route and the Indians it contained was hopelessly hazy. They followed the traditional southern route to California by way of the Arkansas River, crossing the Texas Panhandle into New Mexico and down the Rio Grande Valley, then west to the Pueblo of Tucson. By the time they arrived in Tucson, their equipment was in bad repair, their supplies depleted, and the people themselves drained of their energies. They were urged by the local citizens to remain in Tucson for a

26

few months to replenish equipment and supplies and to renew their strength.

Only one month later, Royce Oatman became restless and wanted to continue west on the last and most trying portion of the trip. He persuaded two families with wagons to join him. They proceeded down the Santa Cruz to the Gila River which they were to follow across two hundred miles of desert to the newly established Fort Yuma, strategically placed at the confluence of the Gila and Colorado rivers.

In the Pima Villages, the Oatman party enjoyed its first real encounter with Arizona Indians. The Pimas were an agricultural people who worked fields of grain and fiber. They were a warm and hospitable tribe, meek, and without hostility. The Oatmans' fellow travelers, the Wilder and Kelly families, elected to remain in the Pima Villages for a few weeks, but Royce Oatman was again uneasy and headed his wagon west for Fort Yuma, still one hundred miles away.

Late in the afternoon of March 19, 1851, the Oatmans made the last camp near the great bend of the Gila River. They were discouraged and exhausted, supplies were low, and they went about their evening chores of preparing food and beds for the night.

Then it happened! Nineteen Indians stood silently in their midst, as if they had erupted from the desert floor. They were sullen and aggressive in their demands for food. Royce Oatman urged his family to continue working while he attempted to placate the Indians. He offered them flour from his meager supply. They took it and demanded more. Oatman told them honestly that supplies were low and he could spare no more.

The Indians withdrew for a council, speaking in their native tongue, then charged the frightened family with knives and clubs. Screams and sobs split the evening air. The low mumbling groans of the mortally wounded added to the terror. In two minutes it was over. The mother, father, and four small children were dead. Sixteen-year-old Lorenzo, having been clubbed senseless, showed some signs of life and he was picked up by three of the attackers and thrown over a rocky bluff onto the river bank. Two young Oatman girls – Mary Ann, age seven

27

and Olive, fifteen, had been taken captive, unharmed, but terrified as they watched the wagon being looted and the bodies of their loved ones searched for valuables. Then, numbed with fear, the young girls watched the pitiful flames of the campfire fade and disappear as the Indians carried them off into the desert night.

In the Oatman Massacre, no specific tribe of Indians was mentioned as having been participants. Popular history has always readily named "Apaches" as the assaulting party. All reliable accounts of the tragedy state the weapons used were knives and clubs. These weapons are not identified with Apache warriors; the bow and arrow, and when available, guns, were the favorite weapons of the Apache nations. Well-informed students of Southwestern tribes suspect the Yavapais were the ones who dispatched the Oatman family. Their theories are based on two significant points. The site of the encounter near the present-day town of Gila Bend was territory well within the Yavapai occupation in 1851. Secondly, knives and clubs were weapons typical of the Yavapais at this time. In all probability, the authorities are correct.

Lorenzo Oatman regained consciousness the following day. Although weak and delirious, he was aware of the tragic sight at the top of the bluff below which he lay. His mother and father and four brothers and sisters were dead. He was also aware that his sisters, Olive and Mary Ann, were now held as captives. He was soon found by two Pima hunters who carried him back to their village, where he was nursed back to health.

The Wilder and Kelly families took him to Fort Yuma, after burying the rest of the Oatman family beside their wagon. The commanding officer of Fort Yuma at the time was a Major Heintzelman, who assumed the girls to be dead and therefore felt it useless to risk additional loss by attempting their recovery. The heartsick, sixteen-year-old Lorenzo was taken to San Francisco to start life anew. Within a year, Olive and Mary Ann were traded to the Mohaves for two horses and a few strings of beads. Mary Ann died while a slave of the tribe.

At Fort Yuma, rumors of the Oatman girls persisted. Indians and traders reported having seen a white girl in a

Mohave camp. Uninformed but active tongues painted outrageous pictures of the fate of the two. Brother Lorenzo appealed to the Bureau of Indian Affairs but his cause was ineffective, weighed down by the reams of government red tape. Rescue seemed more doubtful daily. It was a civilian employee of Fort Yuma, Henry Grinnell, who finally took some direct action. He told a Yuma Indian he had accumulated a great reward of horses, jewelry, food, and blankets if a trade could be arranged with the Mohaves for the return of Olive Oatman. The Indian promised to try, and left at once for the Mohave country. Three weeks later he returned to Fort Yuma and asked Grinnell for the reward. The Indian took him to a grove of willows in the river bottom where Olive Oatman huddled in the brush, naked and sobbing. Henry Grinnell was the first white man she had seen in five years.

The next few weeks of Olive's life were crowded with newspaper interviews, stage appearances, and brutal, insensitive public interrogation. Olive and brother Lorenzo then resumed their education in California, and two years later moved to New York. In 1865, at the age of thirty, Olive married John B. Fairchild, a promising young Rochester attorney. The Fairchilds had three children. Olive Oatman Fairchild died in Sherman, Texas, on March 20, 1903, at the age of seventy-eight.

The blue, line tattoo the Mohaves had inscribed on her chin was a grim and indelible billboard that constantly advertised her five-year ordeal among the Indians. Olive wore it with dignity and royal bearing as if it were a crown of thorns or a symbol of survival.

Camp Verde Cavalry, circa 1964. Photograph courtesy of the Ruffner Collection.

News Value

Every year we observe National Newspaper Week as a reminder of the value of a free press. But newspapers have hundreds of ancillary values which sometimes escape the casual eye. A truly talented individual can find a hundred thrifty uses for a daily paper after its prime function of informing has been exhausted.

During the great depression of the Thirties, a northern Arizona editor received a pitiful plea in his mail one morning. The letter outlined the plight of the writer who was a dry farmer a few miles out of town. The man explained to the editor he had been a victim of the depression as well as the weather. The lack of rain had reduced his crop yield to a few dehydrated stalks and stunted vines. What few pigs he had were lean and bony. His eleven head of cattle looked like fragile wooden frames, barely able to support a red-and-white hide. He was concerned that in the midst of this ordeal, his subscription to the local paper was about to expire. He did not have the money to renew it. He assured the editor, however, that if his subscription was renewed by the paper, he would honor the obligation as soon as his fortunes improved.

The editor was a compassionate man (some are); he answered the letter in the kindest tones and garments of diplomacy. He stated that while credit was not available, barter was an honorable vehicle of practiced economy, and the newspaper had a great need for corn cobs as an excellent tool for cleaning their presses. An exchange could be arranged, a pickup load of corn cobs for a year's subscription to the paper.

In a few days the editor received his answer. It was honest but disappointing. It devastated his professional pride. The farmer stated briefly that he had no corn cobs, and furthermore, if he had any corn cobs, he certainly wouldn't need a subscription to a newspaper.

The Green River Knife

No single Western character made a larger contribution to the opening of the American West than the fur trader. History records the names of some 2,000 mountain men who traversed the pristine wilderness of early America from 1820 to 1840. In this twenty-year-period, the mountain men familiarized themselves with every area of Western America. They alone had the claim to primacy. It was after the mountain men that the U.S. Army explorations came, then the pioneer settlers, the cowboy, and finally, the homesteaders. The fur trader's equipment was as simple as his needs – perhaps a horse, but more often his feet, a bit of jerked meat and hard tack, and his Hawken rifle. But above all, his Green River knife.

The name, Green River, oddly enough, had no connection with the Green River of Wyoming and Utah, which was so well traveled by the mountain men. The name for the knife came from the Green River of Massachusetts upon the banks of which John Russell of Deerfield had built a cutlery factory in 1829. It was here that Russell began to produce the Green River knife which the mountain men cherished. It was a basic butcher knife made of superior steel. The tang extended the full length of the New England hardwood handle. The wood handle itself was unfinished, but large polished brass rivets married the metal and wood. Stamped on the blade, and running from the tip towards the hilt were the words, "J. Russell and Company Green River Works." The personal accounts of mountain men contain a number of references of hand-to-hand combat in which they

33

stated, "I gave him my steel clean up to Green River," indicating the knife had been plunged into his opponent to a great depth. "I gave him 'The Works'" indicated a superior performance. Soon the phrase "up to Green River" became a simile for any job well done.

The records of the Russell Works show that about five to ten thousand of these knives were shipped to the Far West trade each year for about eleven years. They were used by the mountain men as well as traded to the Indians. They became the mountain man's basic tool, never more than an arm's length away from him day and night. They were generally carried in a deep sheath, made and colorfully beaded by the local Indians.

If the Russell records are correct, there were at least 30,000 Green River knives in the West before Samuel Colt produced his first revolver in 1836. It really wasn't a gun that won the West – it was a knife!

A Blast in Boston

Frederick A. Tritle, the sixth territorial governor, is not recalled in the histories of Arizona in the most fervent of terms. He served a near-colorless four years as governor from 1881 to 1885.

While his administration was short on accomplishment, it was also skinny on scandal; both of these facts only added pallor to his public image. Tritle was a native of Pennsylvania, and at the time of his presidential appointment to the Arizona governor's chair, he was a stockbroker in Virginia City, Nevada. The "high point" of Governor Tritle's term occurred at a festive formal dinner in Boston, Massachusetts, in 1883. The governors of several states and territories were being entertained by Governor Bullock of the Great Commonwealth of Massachusetts. It was an elegant affair, liberally tinseled with crystal, linen, silver service, and (if it's the right word) a staggering supply of wine. To suggest that an ex-stockbroker from Virginia City, Nevada, would succumb to such blandishments might be difficult to prove, but it was a possibility.

During the course of that elegant dinner, a gracious guest rose to propose a toast, raising his glistening goblet to Governor Bullock and asking the guests assembled to drink to the Governor of the "Oldest Commonwealth." Before Governor Bullock ever had a chance to respond to the gesture, Arizona's Governor, Frederick A. Tritle, rose to address the distinguished assembly. He thanked the proper Bostonians for the honor rendered him as governor of the Territory of Arizona. He reminded them that Arizona had had a school ably conducted by missionaries long before Harvard had set out its first sprigs of ivy. He called their attention to an order of government and civilization centuries old; the ancient acumen necessary to construct a vast system of irrigation canals was cited; Arizona's heritage of Spanish law, he mentioned, was well established long before the first tea leaves struck the chilled surface of Boston harbor.

When Tritle resumed his seat, the Bostonians and their guest sat in stunned silence. When he returned to Arizona, he was a hero, highly respected and beloved by his constituents. As with all controversial events, it was both delightful and unfortunate. It made great Eastern press.

Whether the Governor's action that evening was prompted by over-indulgence or over-enthusiasm makes little difference; for a brief time, anyway, the eyes of Boston were upon Arizona.

Inn – The Canyon

The resort hotels of Arizona have for years enjoyed a fine reputation throughout the world.

They have made a tremendous impact upon the economy of the state and served to influence thousand of families to adopt Arizona as a permanent home. Names like El Tovar, Camelback Inn, San Marcos, Castle Hot Springs, and Arizona Inn are easily identified by the "snow birds" of the world.

Probably the first purely resort hotel in Arizona was built in 1883 in the bottom of the Grand Canyon. The Farley Hotel, named after its only owner and employee, was located in an oven-like area of the canyon where Diamond Creek flows into the Colorado River.

When the Atlantic and Pacific Railroad commenced service across northern Arizona in 1882, running between Los Angeles and Chicago, Mr. Farley built his rough, lumber hotel in this remote area. He met the trains at Peach Springs, and transported his guest down Peach Springs Wash by buckboard, for 28 bone-splintering miles to his resort on the banks of the Colorado River. With luck and liquid anaesthetic, the journey took about four hours. This trail of tears can still be traversed today by rugged four-wheel-drive vehicles, but caution and judgement are required companions.

The Farley Hotel consisted of a small lobby, dining room, kitchen, four rooms upstairs and four rooms downstairs, together with an ample front porch which overlooked the muddy Colorado. Farley served as chef, room clerk, housekeeper, guide, and bellboy.

This remote resort was in operation between 1883 and 1889 and accommodated 75 to 100 guests a year. Farley abandoned his enterprise in 1889 and it ever since has stood silent. He left the hotel's register with his Indian friend, Johnnie Nelson, at Peach Springs. It contained the names of almost 600 guests with addresses all over the world. A year later the Nelson home burned to the ground and the flames consumed a document of early Arizona which today would have been invaluable as a key to the history of the Grand Canyon area.

The sun still bakes the sandbars and pink stone cliffs where Diamond Creek trickles into the Colorado; but the Farley Hotel is gone. A few rusty square nails and a piece of pulpy board only whisper of Arizona's yesterday.

Editor's Note:

According to a letter written to Budge Ruffner by O. Dock Marston on April 10, 1973:

..."It was Mr. FARLEE who built the hotel at Diamond Creek...It was built at right bank of Peach Springs Wash about 50-100 yards from the point where it joines [sic] Diamond Creek. You can find a can dump and some rocks from the foundation there."

A Single Standard

In the mid-1930s, the icy fingers of the Great Depression began to thaw. Some Navajos in northern Arizona started to sip the nectar of individual enterprise on the white man's terms. A small, family owned bank then operated in Holbrook. Its owners did business the way most Arizona banks did before they started dealing with magnetic tape, punch cards, and serial numbers. Their biggest credit problem was the absolute and total disregard for the passing of time that Indians and cattlemen have always cherished. When the Holbrook bank opened its doors one morning, a young Navajo man walked to the desk of the banker and presented his request for a livestock loan. While totally inexperienced in the business world, the idea of buying cattle, then selling them at a later date to turn a tidy profit, had great appeal to him. The banker was inclined to make the modest loan, but in the accepted method of good banking practice, he asked the Navajo what he had to offer as security or collateral. The Navajo knew not these words.

The kindly and patient banker then explained by asking his client: "Do you own a truck? Have you other livestock? How many horses do you have?" These questions, and the ideas they created disturbed the Navajo. "Security" and "collateral" were big words of the white man which, in the thinking of the Navajo, were fraught with felonious intent. Meager collateral was cited, however, for the loan was granted and the Indian pursued his plan for profit.

A few days before his note was due, the Navajo returned

to the bank. He approached the banker and withdrew from his tight and well-worn Levi's pocket a rather impressive quantity of cash. He paid his note in full and returned a still sizeable wad of bills to his blue denim trousers. The gesture worried the banker, for obviously this amount of money deserved the security of a bank account, not the doubtful protection of a pair of dirty bluejeans worn by a none-too-stable Indian. The banker suggested in rather urgent tones the the remaining money be placed in his bank. The Navajo asked him but one logical question: "How many horses you got?"

A fire pit on Black Mesa on the Navajo Reservation. Photograph courtesy of the Ruffner Collection.

The Kiva

We turned off the paved road and started to climb. The stunted little desert shrubs began to disappear, and gradually taking their place were the hardier specimens of scrub oak, piñon and a few isolated ponderosa pine. Black Mesa is about 7,000 feet high and from its north rim we looked down on the towering monoliths of Monument Valley as if they were toys forgetfully left on the desert floor. The good dirt road continued south to what would be the headquarters of the coal company and the beginning of the slurry line. It was at this point that the landing strip was to be built.

This is an ancient land reverently occupied for centuries by both Navajo and Hopi. Until the road was built, this land had

41

never known machinery. It was the mother of two great resources: intriguing prehistoric sites which could add much to man's understanding of the cultures which preceded his, and vast deposits of coal to create the energy for which modern man seems to have an insatiable appetite. The Federal Antiquities Law requires that a significant prehistoric site be professionally excavated and analyzed before it is obliterated to meet the demands of an expanding society. Large mining and utility companies know this and faithfully comply.

While the preliminary work for the company's landing strip was being done on Black Mesa, evidence of a large underground kiva appeared directly in the path of the proposed runway. The archaeologists were called in to hurriedly dig, analyze, and record the kiva's relationship to another time. It was this final sight we had journeyed to see, before the gravel pall of runway had sealed it from all eyes forever.

The chalky dust billowed from beneath our tires as we drove over the recently disturbed earth. We parked a few yards from the open kiva and, sheltering our cameras from the settling dust, walked to the edge of the excavation. Two Navajo laborers were brushing away the soil from the last corrugated storage vessel. Squatting in the dirt, they whispered their admiration of its beauty and mystery, then cradling it in their arms, they carried it up the ladder and away from the kiva as if it were a sick child. The pot was photographed, identified, and placed in the archaeologist's carryall. The kiva itself was then thoroughly photographed and measured, its dimensions recorded.

The mining company foreman was told that the excavation was complete; it could now be covered by the new earth and the airstrip construction could proceed. The huge bulldozer aimed at the open kiva, lowered its giant blade and pushed a breaker of dirt toward the opening. We stood silently as the first wave of earth thumped into the ancient sanctuary. The Indians turned and walked away. Something of value had been lost, another value adopted.

First Passage?

The Colorado River has generated as much romantic controversy as it has kilowatt hours. Major John Wesley Powell, a one-armed Civil War veteran, is credited by most historians with being the first man to navigate the river the entire length of the Grand Canyon. A hundred years later there remains a substantial shadow on his claim. The Major's first expedition on the Colorado River took place in 1869. On September 14, 1867, two full years before Powell's well-publicized journey, the following news story appeared in *The Arizona Miner*, published in Prescott by John H. Marion, Editor:

Navigation of the Big Cañon
A Terrible Voyage

William J. Beggs, who arrived here today from Hardyville, brings us the following account of the first passage, so far as is known of any human being through the Big Cañon of the Colorado. He derived the particulars from Captain Wilburn of the Barge Colorado, who arrived at Hardyville on Monday last, and James Ferry of Callville, who arrived on Tuesday:

In April last a party, consisting of Captain Baker, an old Colorado prospector and formerly a resident of St. Louis, George Strobe, also from St. Louis, and James White, formerly of Penosha, Iowa, and late of Company H, Fifth California Cavalry, left Colorado City to prospect on San Juan River, which empties into the Colorado between the junction of Green and Grand Rivers and the Big Cañon. They prospected until the middle of August with satisfactory success, and then decided to return to Colorado City for a supply of provisions and a larger company. They set out to go by the mouth of the San Juan, with the double purpose of finding a more practicable route to Green River than the one they had traversed, and of visiting some localities which Captain Baker had prospected some years previously. On the morning of the 24th of August, while encamped about a mile from the Colorado, they were attacked by a band of about fifty′ Utes. Captain Baker was killed, but Strobe and White secured their carbines and revolvers, some rope and a sack containing ten pounds of flour, and ran to the Colorado, where they found a few small drift logs, which they hastily lashed together, and embarking on the frail raft, started down the river in the hope of reaching Callville. On the second day, they came to the first rapids, in passing over which they lost their flour. On the third day, they went over a fall ten feet high, and Strobe was washed from the raft and drowned. White had lashed himself to the raft, which although shattered by the shock, sustained him, and he hauled it up on an island below the fall, repaired it, and proceeded alone. He had not much hope of getting through alive, but he thought his body might go through, and being found, furnish a clue by which his friends might learn his fate. He describes the course of the river as very tortuous, with a constant succession of rapids and falls, the latter varying in height from four to ten or twelve feet. Sometimes when he plunged over a fall the raft would turn over upon him, and he would have much difficulty in extricating himself from his perilous position. For a few days he found on bars and islands in the river sufficient mezquit [sic] to allay the pangs of hunger, but for seven days he had nothing to eat but a leather knife scabbard. He saw a few lizards but was unable to catch them; and he looked from side to side in vain for any mode of egress from the cañon, the perpendicular walls of which were in many places a mile and a half, as well as he could estimate, in height.

He floated on an average, about ten hours a day, hauling up at night on the bars which were formed by the eddies below the falls. For about ten days he was without hat, pants or boots, having lost them while going over a fall. On the afternoon of the 6th inst. he passed the mouth of the Virgin River, and a party of Pah-Utes swam off and pushed his raft ashore. They stole one of two pistols which he had managed to preserve, and he bartered the other to them for the hind quarters of a dog, one of which he ate for supper and the other for breakfast. On the 7th he reached Callville, and was taken care of by Captain Wilburn and Mr. Ferry. He was much emaciated, his legs and feet were blistered and blackened by the sun; his hair and beard, which had been dark, were turned white, and he walked with difficulty, being unable to stand erect. . . .

From his actual traveling time, and the rapidity of the current, it is estimated the distance through the cañon, from the mouth of the San Juan to Callville, is not much short of five hundred miles.

This would mean, then, in today's geography, that the frail little raft of James White took him from the upper reaches of the present-day Lake Powell through the Grand Canyon to what is now Lake Mead. This story, and hundreds of other versions of it, sparked the controversy which has smoldered for a century.

James White died on January 14, 1927, at the age of 89, after having lived a long and unblemished life. Both White and Powell have had their detractors and advocates. Today, the ruins of Callville lie beneath the watery canopy of Lake Mead, and the mortal remains of James White sleep beneath the soil of the Odd Fellows Cemetery, in Trinidad, Colorado. Only the question and the river remain.

One Hell of a Tank

When a man's roots have crept into the soil of one small area of Arizona for about three-quarters of a century, he may become a bit provincial. Toughy Peach was in his teens and living in Camp Verde when news of Geronimo's death reached that lovely little river town in February, 1909. In later years Toughy could recall the admission of Arizona to the Union, and a hundred other events crisply printed on the pages of Arizona history. Some of the best cattle country in Arizona was his playpen and he grew into manhood riding horseback from the cottonwoods along the banks of the Verde River to the grassy slopes of the Mogollon Rim.

This country and its cattle shaped his mind and body; he was a cowboy. He always had been. From the time he was a small boy, his complete planning and thinking had been in this direction. To Toughy, it was unthinkable that a man should want to spend his life anywhere but on a cow ranch.

The repair of the fences, the condition of the range grass, rain or the lack of it, how near full or empty the water holes and cattle tanks are – these were the things which had real meaning to Toughy Peach. Here the amount of available water determines the economy. Water means security. Dryness and drought portend disaster and ruin. In his lifetime, Toughy had ridden hundreds of miles, to check the level of various cattle tanks, and these were the bodies of water he was most familiar with.

In the summer of 1963, Toughy took one of his few trips beyond the borders of his own Arizona. The Camp Verde

Cavalry, to which he belonged, was to appear in a parade in Santa Barbara, California, and he looked forward not only to the parade and fiesta, but primarily to see first-hand the Pacific Ocean. A sea of this size had really been more of a legend than a reality to Toughy. He sat patiently beside the driver of the automobile all night as they crossed the vast California desert and threaded through the freeway system toward Santa Barbara and the sea.

It was a beautiful coastal morning when the car carrying Toughy rounded a sweeping section of freeway and there before him was a magnificent panoramic view of the Pacific Ocean. He stared at its size, unbelieving, but his comment brought it into cowboy focus:

"Yup, she's up."

Color and Command

Colonel Emelio Kosterlitzsky was the type of man that legend seems to encrust, like the barnacles on a weary ship. A colonel in the Rurales, the early day federal police of Mexico, his career with this punitive organization lasted some forty years. Known in police circles as "Kosterlitzsky the constipated Cossack," he was educated in various military schools in Poland and Russia. While a young officer in service of the Russian Czar, he had suffered the professional soldier's two most traumatic experiences: disappointment in love, and defeat in battle. His next move was America, and here his history is blurred. One theory is that he jumped ship in New York harbor and took an American vessel to Guaymas to join the Mexican Army. Most histories state that he deserted from the 6th United States Cavalry at Fort Apache, Arizona in 1872, and fled to Mexico. His U.S. rank of corporal was, in his opinion, beneath the dignity of a comprehensive military education and an insult to his aristocratic birth.

When he joined the Mexican Army, he was commissioned a captain and rose quickly to lieutenant colonel, and ultimately became a full colonel. His steel-gray hair was Prussian cropped, and his elegant mustache meticulously manicured even when he had spent days in the saddle in the vastnesses of northern Sonora. His instinctive military bearing served to display his elaborate and well-tailored uniforms. By his side a saber swung, a constant reminder of command. His troops were taut and tough, serving the multiple purposes of police, prosecutors, and executioners. There was no appeal from their decisions, no avenue of escape from their accusations. When the Rurales chose to hang an offending peon, a black-braided rope was used. The same type of rope formed the uniform hat-band of Kosterlitzsky's troops, worn proudly on their sombreros. It created an organizational image of somber quality. On one occasion, an American lady living near the border casually mentioned her anxieties to the gallant Colonel. He answered her with his usual flair: "My dear, should you be molested, pray notify me. I shall order my men to kill whomever annoys you."

In 1913, the Villa revolutionists brought about the fall of President Días. Kosterlitzsky, with a small contingent of his troops, rode toward the Arizona border to seek asylum. Nearing Nogales, Arizona, they met a huge crowd of revolutionists, jeering them in their defeat. Always the soldier, Kosterlitzsky ordered a Cossack-type saber charge through the taunting mob. He literally hacked his way through a barrier of flesh and bone to the International border, then formally surrendered his bloody saber to the United States Army at Nogales. While some historians state that this was not the method of his escape, equally eminent historians suggest that this style was typical of the man.

The colorful soldier spent his last years as a retired gentleman in southern California. Though he never again crossed the Mexican border, he was a frequent visitor in the homes of many Arizona lawmen who had been his lifelong friends. In 1927, Kosterlitzsky was buried beneath the green grass of California, his saber at his side.

The Scalpers

A few years prior to the Mexican War, Apache problems became a capital concern of the Mexican government. The governors of Chihuahua and Sonora, seeking a deterrent, placed a thirty dollar bounty on each Apache scalp checked into the authorities. This Pandoric proclamation unleashed upon the Indians of the Southwest one of the most grisly onslaughts in history. From under the wet rocks of the wilderness crept the scalp hunters.

One of these emerging personalities was John Gallintin, a waste product of the Santa Fe Trail, whose limited talents readily adapted him to this endeavor. He formed a brigade of some twenty men and combed the mountains and deserts for the black hair of the Apaches. Some success was immediate, but the Apache grew increasingly difficult to locate and Gallintin began to pad his deficits with Cocopa, Yuma, Navajo, Papago, Pima, and even the jet-black hair of the citizens of Mexico.

Once this inhumane fraud was detected, Gallintin retreated to the isolation of northern New Mexico. By the time the Mexican War was over, John Gallintin had collected, by one means or the other, about 3,000 head of sheep, with which he left New Mexico in 1849 to corner the mutton market in the California gold fields.

By January, 1850, Gallintin's group of seventeen men were with their sheep, nearing the Colorado River at Fort Yuma. When they were making camp for the night, a number of Yuma Indians appeared unarmed and began to bring in wood for the fires. Inasmuch as they showed no signs of hostility, they were permitted to remain in camp and enjoy the heat of the blaze. The Yumas put long cottonwood poles on all four fires, placing the center of the poles in the center of the fires. When the last pole had burned through the middle – creating two fiery clubs – an Indian screamed as a signal. The Yumas picked up the clubs and dispatched John Gallintin and his helpers to the not-too-happy hunting ground. Three thousand sheep were the spoils of the Yumas!

John Gallintin had failed to remember – that elephants and Indians never forget a face.

Dick's Appomattox

He was an old man when he died – a very old man. With his brother he ran a typical country store in the desert community of Congress Junction in southern Yavapai County. The store was a frame building sanded smooth by the desert wind. Its tin roof was rusted to a rich brown. Inside was a mercantile museum. Much of the inventory was hung from the rafters; kerosene lanterns and granite bowls swayed above saddle blankets stacked on the floor. Bales of hay and sacks of sheep salt were stored in a small anteroom which reflected the architecture of an afterthought. On the rough-sawn shelves stood the spices of the world's exotic trade routes, together with Arbuckle's coffee, Longhorn cheese and dried peaches. Assorted sizes of steel traps were strung from the center post. This was the emporium of the Bullard Brothers.

Both of the brothers had been soldiers in the cause of the Confederacy. Both had come to Arizona a few years after the War Between the States to escape the hardship and the hostility which still festered in the South. In the clean desert air of central Arizona, William seemed to forget the bitterness of the conflict in which he had engaged. Dick never did. Those who knew him religiously avoided any discussion of the Civil War. Those who did blunder into the subject were shocked by his emotional reaction. His voice would become shrill, his eyes enlarge, the veins of his neck would stand out in deep relief and pulsate. He felt that he had been betrayed by his own comrades in arms.

The South had not met defeat in his mind – it had

squandered the victory. Dick generally concluded his tirade on these occasions with a charge which achieved a degree of regional immortality.

"Ah nevah surrendered. Robert E. Lee surrendered, but ah nevah surrendered. Ah was a sharpshooter, by God!"

The Civil War of Dick Bullard wasn't concluded that Palm Sunday in 1865 at Appomattox Courthouse. Dick's war wasn't over until 1931 when the old man slipped into sleep underneath a palo verde tree on Martinez Wash.

The Bon Vivant

His name has been mercifully misplaced. He was a large, raw-boned man who had been all over the world in the practice of his profession. Constant travel and periodic residence in the exotic corners of the globe had sharpened his sophistication. He enjoyed "the good life" and his ability to live it had become a fine art.

It must have been a shock when, in the prime of his life, his company sent him to the embryonic village of Clarkdale, Arizona, to design and construct a smelter. An engineer whose talents in this field were much in demand, he had enjoyed assignments in Peru, Europe, and the Middle East; his family generally accompanied him, but in this case, it was out of the question.

In 1912, the town had barely been started, and even the basic amenities of life were as yet on the horizon; it would be years, a century perhaps, before a full urban life might be lived on the high desert of Arizona. He left New York City without family or friends and journeyed west to what he knew was a hellhole.

The demand of his work was the only anesthesia available to him those several months he lived in Clarkdale. The food was basic boarding house and the pool hall the cultural center of the community. A cold beer was revered with the same awe as a three foot piece of the true Cross. But finally the ordeal was over, his work was done. He journeyed to Ash Fork and boarded the finest Santa Fe train headed east to the centers of civilized living.

When he went into the diner that night the sights and smells of a former life greeted him. Downy white linen on the table; silver service, crystal decanters, a bud vase with a rose, and the menu included his favorite: raw oysters. It seemed as if ages had passed since he had enjoyed this delicacy. He requested the waiter to bring him a dozen and asked that when he observed these had been consumed, he repeat the order.

Four times the old waiter placed a dozen raw oysters in front of the engineer before his curiosity forced him to comment. "Sir," he said, as he removed from the table the fourth plate of empty oyster shells, "are you goin' home or leavin' home?"

It seemed a most logical question.

The Name Arizona

In 1854, the Territory of New Mexico memorialized the United States Congress to create a separate territory from its vast expanse to ease the widely distributed burden of local government. Three names were suggested for the new territory: "Pimería," "Gadsonia" and, fortunately, "Arizona." The last was chosen for its euphonious appeal.

At the time, no one bothered to inquire as to the roots and meaning of the newly selected name. Perhaps it was just as well, for in the century to come, numerous individuals with varying degrees of qualification were to speculate frequently regarding the meaning of the word.

Reports in Spanish archives refer to the "District of Arizona" in speaking of the northern portion of what was then still in Sonora, and what is now a portion of Pima County. Spanish discoveries of ore in the mid-eighteenth century, near the present day Arivaca, Arizona, were sent from a shipping point the Spanish called "Arizonac" to Mexico City. This name is said to be derived from the Papago word *"ali"* (small) and *"shonak"* (place of the spring) – the composite, "place of the small spring."

The revered historian Bancroft suggested the name came about as the result of the shape of the area of the Gadsden Purchase. To one possessing a lucid imagination, the Gadsden Purchase was shaped somewhat like a nose. Bancroft advocated the Spanish "nariz" in the form "Narizona" or "Largenose Woman." The idea is, of course, most unflattering to both the state and all womanhood. The most common theory cites the Spanish word "arida" (arid, dry, barren), and the suffix "zona" (zone). Many students of Spanish, however, have doubts about this origin.

The source of the name of the Valentine State is virtually impossible to prove. The Papago "ali-shonak" (place of small spring) seems to have more learned advocates as well as more plausibility. It is an odds-on favorite.

When Senator Rush of Texas presented the New Mexico memorial to Congress in 1854, the wording called for the creating of the "Territory of Arizona." Charles D. Poston, "The Father of Arizona," stated this was, to his knowledge, the first time the word "Arizona" was used in an official United States Government document. We should be grateful the name persisted; being a resident of Gadsonia could be pretty unimpressive.

Public Health

It was a very delicate situation and the old doctor knew it. This was the type of thing that made him regret he had ever agreed to serve as county health officer. It was a fact, however, and he had to deal with it. If it were handled too openly, if too much were made of it, there would be severe economic implications for the town. Then, too, there would be that segment of the community which would find it offensive; the health of the town, however, had to be maintained.

At any cost, outright panic must be averted, he thought. It would be a mistake to make a public announcement, but the menace itself had to be contained. He knew this type of health problem should not become common knowledge; it would embarrass the county attorney and the sheriff, the city administration and, oh, so many who pretended the impossibility of such a development. The unsuspecting public must be protected.

"The girls" themselves were no problem. They eagerly sought the medical attention which would return them to, at least, an economically fruitful life. A garish red quarantine sign on the front door was bound to look bad; it would be blunt and frightening and have an impact on the Prescott public which could not be quickly erased.

A diplomatic, even euphemistic, type of poster was the only answer, the doctor concluded; worded to discourage a prospective patron, yet with no implication of hazard to health or morals. The old man sat down at his roll-top desk, moistened his cigar, and, in his Tennessee pace, methodically printed the sign with a black crayon.

When he finished he carried it down Gurley Street, one block west of the Plaza, to the brothel and tacked it to the front door of the old brick building. Only three words but it told the story:

CLOSED FOR REPAIRS.

The Promoter

The history of Arizona is fraught with incidents of real-estate fraud. This type of promotion is usually conceived in the shadows of deceit and swaddled in a linen of lies. One such fraud as this, however, started out half in jest and eventually created one of Arizona's most progressive cities. Following the Gadsden Purchase in 1854, the area where the city of Yuma now stands became American soil. There was no town at this location; only one house stood on the California side of the river which housed the operator of the only ferry on this portion of the river. The ferryman was Don D. Jaeger, an ambitious German immigrant, whose hefty ferry fees compensated him well for the lonely life he lived at this desert river crossing. In 1850 he had carried 60,000 souls from bank to bank as a result of the great travel caused by the discovery of gold in California. He dreamed, however, not of a fortune made in the ferry business, but rather of the great potential of the raw land.

In February, 1855, the "Father of Arizona" Charles D. Poston, with his faithful band of employees, appeared on the east bank of the river enroute to California. Poston was a mining promoter and therefore broke. He hoped, however, to remedy this situation by a trip to the gold fields where money for mining development seemed to be inexhaustible. The eager business man, Jaeger, quoted forty dollars to take the Poston men and equipment over to the California side of the muddy stream. Poston feigned disinterest in the crossing and sent his crew into the flat desert land which bordered the east side of the river.

Soon a survey party headed by Poston's engineer, Herman Ehrenberg, was absorbed in the laying out of a town. Transits, signal flags, and chain crews attracted the ferryman's attention. He crossed the river and began to interrogate the workmen regarding their reason for such a survey. Each man declined comment and referred him to Mr. Poston for information and thus set the scene for swindle. In hushed tones, Poston swore Jaeger to secrecy and told him of great plans of eastern industrialists to develop a city on this strategic spot of desert.

The colorful con artist Poston painted a glowing panorama of instant metropolis. Mesmerized by Poston's presentation, the ferryman pleaded for purchase privileges. Of course, as a special concession, it was granted, and almost as an afterthought, ferriage fees were taken as down payment for a choice lot.

Charles D. Poston was indeed an Arizona pioneer; what a pity the fifty-dollar-down set who today sell slices of Malapai Meadows, couldn't have seen him operate. The city of Yuma stands today, a testament to his vision and salesmanship. It might never have been there at all had he just paid the ferry fee and gone on his way.

Situation Ethics on the Santa Cruz

There are those who still wonder why he was called "The Father of Arizona." To the quick-frozen dehydrated historian, and there are many of them, the title was bestowed because of Poston's hyperactive efforts on behalf of Territorial status for Arizona. There may be, however, another reason for the designation.

At one time in his colorful career, Charles D. Poston was the *alcalde* (mayor) of the tiny settlement of Tubac in the Santa Cruz River Valley. In this pre-Civil War period most of Tubac's population was Mexican, for very few Anglos sought such a stark environment. Poston, feeling the heady wind of public office, took it upon himself to legalize a number of loosely structured living arrangements which he had observed among a number of the citizens in the village.

The priest for Tubac lived in Altar in northern Sonora. (At this period in history, the entire area was under a single Church government.) Because of the distance and difficulty involved he seldom came to Tubac to perform the various functions of his office. Poston, unaware that this arrangement had existed for years, began to act on the capacity of a magistrate and started to marry various couples whom the housing shortage and impatient chemistry had forced into a "meaningful relationship." He performed the service at no charge and even gave the bride five silver dollars to establish a dowry.

In the primitive desert village where both money and recreation were at a premium, the idea had a great deal of appeal. Many of the couples named their offspring after Poston. In time the priest from Altar arrived to minister to the members of his satellite parish. When he became aware of what had happened, he was enraged and excommunicated all who had engaged in such civil frivolity. Poston, being both a sensitive and intelligent man, felt a keen responsibility for the religious plight of his people.

He set to work at once to remedy the cultural dislocations which he had inadvertently caused. In his later writings he stated that this well-intended activity had cost him several days of constant persuasion plus $500 in cold hard cash. Apparently, his Christian charity prevented him from detailing the procedure in his book *Apache Land*. The priest finally agreed to remarry all those in question and Poston, the well-meaning *alcalde* of Tubac, declared a one-day fiesta which was concluded with a *Gran Baile* that evening. It was a magnificent event. The children were invited.

A Crusading Editor

Most historians agree that the first newspaper published within the borders of present-day Arizona was the *Weekly Arizonian* which first appeared at Tubac in March, 1859. There are those, of course, who disagree, for this is a profession which is not renowned for unanimity.

It is also generally conceded that the first newspaper to be published in northern Arizona was the *Arizona Miner,* datelined Fort Whipple, Arizona Territory, March 8, 1864. The editor was the flamboyant Tisdale A. Hand, fat on flowery phrases, woefully thin on factual presentation. At that date Fort Whipple was located near Del Rio Springs, located some thirty miles north of present-day Prescott. The motto of the *Arizona Miner* was "The Gold of the Land is Good." Ironic, isn't it, that the land hucksters of Chino Valley have the same thought a century later?

The revered historian James H. McClintock in his *History of Arizona,* published in 1916, suggests that the *Arizona Miner* was indeed not the first newspaper published in northern Arizona. McClintock cites the Army activity on the Colorado River some years before the creation of the Arizona Territory. Fort Mojave served as an important base in the area and here, he states, three men – Dr. John J. Milhau, an Army surgeon; Montgomery Bryant; and Post Trader Peter R. Brady – organized and published the first newspaper in northern Arizona, the fast-fading *Mojave Dog Star.*

Started as a lark, it died a lark's death. The entire

motivation of the founders of the *Mojave Dog Star* was to mass an editorial campaign to "correct" the free-love tendencies of the Mojave Indians. Those of us who are firm believers in cultural integrity can only be grateful for the failure of such a short-sighted and envious editorial policy.

Prescott Frontier Days Rodeo, 1958. Photograph courtesy of the Ruffner Collection.

It Takes Time

There aren't many like him left. Quiet, but not without humor, and just enough meat on his frame to round out the legs of his Levi's.

I was sitting underneath a big juniper tree when he drove up. What had been a dry wash now ran bank to bank, severing the dirt road with a roaring ribbon of dirty water; until it receded, our separate journeys had ended. He squatted on his boot heels and we started the trivial talk the occasion demanded. The weather: how dry the country had been and how grateful we were for the rain. The creek went down some, but its volume of flow still forced more time-killing conversation. He mentioned a favorite book he had bought in 1939 and how much he had enjoyed it.

It had been a source of discussion on many bunkhouse nights or when he was out someplace on the ranch with the wagon. Most of the cowboys he worked with had read it. He talked about it.

"About a year before Pearl Harbor I lent the book to an ol' boy who was workin' for an outfit at Camp Wood. He was batchin' there that winter and told me he would like to read it and return it to me. I went to his wedding at Skull Valley in 1948 but didn't think to ask him about it. A few years later I saw his oldest boy at the 4-H calf sale in Prescott; he told me he thought he had seen the book around the house and would try and remember to ask his dad about it, but I never heard no more about it. In 1960, we hired a fella from Peach Springs to help us work the fall roundup and he knew this guy I had lent the book to. He told me he thought his first wife had left him but he had married again and was running a little outfit for someone down around Kirkland. I don't get down around there very often, but I figured I might see him in town someday and ask him about it. I sure didn't want him to lose that book.

"The next year I spotted him at the Labor Day Rodeo in Williams. He was back of the buckin' chutes, but by the time I got over there he was nowhere in sight. I saw his ex-wife on The Row one night and she told me she was sure he had took the book with him when they had 'split the blanket.' It was December, wasn't it? Nineteen and sixty-seven when the big snow hit? A fella came through the ranch one day about a month later, with the county road grader. He told me the ol' boy who borrowed the book from me had moved back to Camp Wood and was working at the old Hill place. I think it was almost the end of June when I got a chance to get over there. I found him out on one of them granite ridges building fence. We talked awhile, then finally I got around to askin' him if he remembered borrowin' the book from me. He said he sure did and he thought old Mr. Favour had wrote it real well and he sure did respect old Bill Williams who Mr. Favour had writ about, and how interesting it was. 'Well, when are you going to return it?' I asked him.

"'Just as soon as I finish it,' he said."

The water was low now, we walked back to our cars and eased them down the sloping bank and into the rocky water. I followed his car on up the hill through the cedars, moving again towards my destination. Twenty-nine years had passed. What a beautiful way to wait for a creek to go down.

In 1995, Prescott's Frontier Days Rodeo parade had as its grand marshal, Ben Johnson, and – for the first time – an honorary grand marshal, Budge Ruffner.

Ben Johnson (the only American to win both an Academy Award and the title of World Champion Cowboy) was best remembered in Prescott for his supporting role in "Junior Bonner" – his last Arizona western, filmed there in 1971. The movie catering truck was set up in the Ruffner Funeral Home's parking lot where Budge shared many lunch hours with Ben and the other cast members.

"Junior Bonner"'s storyline centered around the Prescott rodeo and Budge and his family were closely connected with the rodeo. His uncle, George, helped organize and stage Prescott's rodeo in 1888 and in 1897 was the first man in the Arizona Territory to "bulldog" a steer. He served as arena director, judge, timer, and carried the American flag at the head of the rodeo parade each year, the last time in 1933 at the age of seventy.

Budge's father, Lester Lee, was arena director from 1913 to 1940. He helped codify the "Prescott rules" and was announcer, finance director, as well as rodeo and parade chairman. As a very young child, Budge rode in rodeo parades seated in the saddle in front of his father until the age of six when he began riding alone. At seven, Budge began participating in Junior rodeo events, riding wild calves.

Here Budge is shown with family members (seated right to left in the surrey) daughter Rebecca, grandson Daniel, wife Elisabeth, and Budge.

Photograph courtesy of the Ruffner Collection.

Prospector's Faith

Around the turn of the century, the hills and mountains of Arizona were pockmarked with mining claims. Their sides and gullies, ledges and escarpments were coated with the offal of the exploration tunnels. An army of prospectors with a faith that bordered on frenzy had penetrated every cranny of the state. Occasionally, some Eastern capital syndicate, its vision blurred by the glorious glow of the Golden West, would express interest in purchasing a mine in these well-worn mountains of Arizona.

One such Boston group came to Arizona about 1900 to investigate a property in the Groom Creek area of the Bradshaw Mountains. It was owned by an old prospector who saw in this negotiation the possibility of retirement in luxury. Before the prospective buyers arrived, the overanxious old miner had used the classic method of "salting" the mine with a shotgun to bolster what he knew to be its marginal quality. He did it himself, alone and unaided. He used 12-gauge shotgun shells with primer and powder in place; none of the usual lead shot was added. Instead of shot, fine placer gold was placed in the shell and fired from the shotgun into likely looking ledges within the mine. He was thorough, diligent, and completely dishonest.

The Boston dandies arrived, accompanied by a young man who had recently graduated from Yale with a virginal degree in mining engineering. The mine was inspected by the young engineer and samples of the salted ore were taken to be assayed. The property was thoroughly scrutinized and the dudes made but one mistake – they showed the old prospector the glowing assay reports.

Arizona prospectors, when it came to gold mines, had the kind of faith that would make a Buddhist monk look like an infidel. Having that kind of faith, he did the only thing he could do. He refused to sell.

An Early Arizona Industry

By 1914, the feather merchants of Phoenix had cornered the market. Of the ten thousand ostriches in the United States at that time, six thousand of them were in the Salt River Valley. Ostrich feathers were in great demand in the fashion centers of the world. Every well-dressed lady had such plumes to decorate her hats. Some wore ostrich-feather capes; and even dresses were embellished with the bloom of these birds. It was a booming business in the Valley and New York buyers were pleading for more production.

Josiah Harbert brought the first pair of birds to Arizona in 1887, together with fourteen chicks. Natives of Africa, the birds thrived in the dry, warm climate of Arizona's desert. An adult ostrich weighed as much as 350 pounds, and stood seven to eight feet tall. The ostrich had a digestive system as efficient and uncomplicated as a garden hose, and grazed on alfalfa and other native grasses with additions of maize and crushed bone to aid in shell production for the eggs. Every six to eight months the birds' mature feathers were stripped from them; the yield from this operation was usually worth $150 to $200 on the open market. A good bird could produce at least $300 a year in feathers and on the basis of six thousand birds, this made its impression on the economy of Phoenix.

The ostrich, however, did have some personal habits which presented problems to the handlers. His kick had a comparable velocity to that of a healthy mule and was far more accurate. These birds lashed out with their huge drumsticks not to the rear, but forward and down in frequent and unprovoked attacks upon their herdsmen. A broken leg was a common occupational hazard for an ostrich farmer. They had the alarming habit of gulping down any shiny metal objects they happened to come upon; a short strand of barb wire, for example, was a favorite; this proved to be somewhat more difficult for them to digest than a chicken enchilada, and frequently caused their demise as well as the loss of a $250 investment for the owner. While they were incapable of flight, they could run at speeds up to 35 miles per hours, and this proved difficult for even an Arizona cowboy to cope with. They were productive, however, for they laid about thirty eggs a year and managed to hatch approximately half of them; the chicks were the size of a full-grown chicken and had a market value of $100. The harvesting of the feathers was accomplished by corralling the birds and placing stockings over their heads, which seemed to calm them, making the process relatively easy once the bird was caught and blinded.

The owners of various ostrich farms formed the Arizona Ostrich Association in 1913, hoping to control the market and protect their investments. Ostrich feathers were still very much in style. The thought that a style change might occur apparently never entered their minds. The main concern among the farmers seemed to be price and production.

Every serious farmer owning birds in the Salt River Valley joined the Association, with one exception. The Pima Indian Council, with headquarters at Sacaton, owned twelve birds. They saw no advantage in membership in a white man's group. Certainly, recent experience with the Anglo had indicated his lack of concern for the future of the Pima Nation, so they chose to operate their ostrich enterprise free from paleface intervention.

The driving force in the Arizona Ostrich Association was Dr. A.J. Chandler of Chandler. His farm, much of which became the grounds of the San Marcos Hotel, ran almost four hundred of the strange birds. The Pan-American Ostrich Company of Phoenix was the largest operator, having a remuda of some twenty-five hundred of the non-flying fowls. Three practicing physicians (doctors seem to be attracted to exotic investments) owned 150 of the feathered debentures. The Belgo-American Ostrich Company was a large operation, with 850 in the hand. The Ellsworth Brothers of Mesa barely got in the business with four of the ungainly creatures. There were a number of other farmers with from 25 to 250 birds.

What caused the failure of this industry? As in most disasters, it wasn't a single cause but a cumulative effect of a number of minor circumstances. The farmers insisted on selling as a group to the New York buyers, rather than negotiating a price on an individual basis. The cost of raw desert land began to rise from a few dollars to nearly $100 an acre. Water for the alfalfa fields became increasingly more difficult to obtain, and membership in an irrigation district was a necessity.

The final blow was, of course, predictable. Fashion changed. Fashion always changes, and this lesson the farmers learned too late. Where previously the feathers an ostrich produced in a year were worth $300, the price drop indicated 10 percent of that amount. The business was doomed. Many birds were sold to zoos or given away; hundreds more were destroyed – their huge skeletons still lie beneath the desert floor to confound future archaeologists.

About twenty years after the passing of the ostrich business in the Salt River Valley, Sally Rand introduced the fan dance at the San Francisco World's Fair. In spite of her use of ostrich-feather fans, the business never really boomed again. The audience reaction toward the fans of Miss Rand was one of resentment rather that appreciation, and the feathers maintained their form better than Sally. History has taught us again and again that most fashions run full circle and will return to their past favor. A smart young man might do well to keep an eye on the ostrich market.

Elisabeth and Budge Ruffner at the Prescott Centennial Ball, held on December 28, 1963. Photograph courtesy of the Ruffner Collection.

Lieutenant Libertine

One of the most colorful characters of the early American period of Arizona history was the bon vivant Lieutenant Sylvester Mowry. For openers: he was from an aristocratic southern family, a West Point graduate who was transferred by his commanding officer from Salt Lake City to Fort Yuma in the early 1850s for attempted seduction of a fellow officer's lady. Being familiar with Sylvester's track record from that point until the end of his life, I suspect the word "attempted" was a charitable addition to the charge to protect the lady's image.

Soon after he arrived at Fort Yuma, Mowry established his quarters and surrounded himself with what frugal facilities the area offered. He quickly learned the joys to be gained by commerce in trade beads, then turned his talents toward the more lasting rewards the gold mines of the region could offer. Taking leave from the Army (a request I am sure they were delighted to honor), Lt. Mowry became deeply involved in local politics and mining promotion.

Edward E. Cross was, at the time, editor of the *Weekly Arizonian,* a weekly newspaper published at Tubac. Editors of weeklies are, of course, notoriously testy. On top of this he was a New England yankee not sympathetic with states' rights philosophies, a conservative with federalist leanings who frequently expressed in the editorial pages of the *Arizonian* his disapproval of Sylvester Mowry's manners, morals, and methods of doing things.

This type of editorial comment tended to create a

somewhat strained relationship between the two men. After a particularly scathing editorial attack in which Cross defined Mowry's pedigree in rather explicit terms, Mowry challenged Cross to a duel with rifles as the weapons. At the appointed time the two men met on the field of honor, a small clearing surrounded by mesquite on the outskirts of town. Cross won the flip of the coin and chose to place Mowry with the desert sun shining in his face. Both men missed their first shot; Cross missed with his second, and Mowry's rifle failed to discharge. True to the code, Mowry was permitted to reprime his weapon, did so and cooly placed the defenseless Cross in his sights. Cross stood erect, his folded arms cradling his rifle, facing his adversary and sure death. Both men froze in this stance for what must have seemed an eternity. Then playing the role of the Southern aristocrat to the hilt, Mowry raised his gun toward the sky and fired. In this, the most famous duel in Arizona history, no blood was let, no dignity damaged, no courage questioned. The tension was relieved. For what happened immediately following the incident, the same cannot be said. The two men, followed by their friends, walked to the town store and took delivery on a forty-two-gallon barrel of prime liquor that had been thoughtfully purchased a few days before. It was then the real mayhem started. Symbolic blood was spilled, dignity dissolved, courage crumbled.

Edward E. Cross soon after sold the *Arizonian* to Sylvester Mowry. He later became a Union officer and died on the field at Gettysburg. On August 24, 1863, the Southern sympathizer Mowry was arrested by Union soldiers for "aiding and abetting the enemy." He was placed in prison where he first arrived in Arizona a decade before, at Fort Yuma. Following the Civil War, Sylvester Mowry, the West Point graduate, collected $40,000 damages from his government and sailed for Europe. He made his home in London and died in that city a short time later, his body riddled, not with wounds, but diseases that his physicians attributed to the indiscretions of his youth.

The Ringer

When the first calf is released from the roping chute at the local rodeo, one of the toughest competitive sporting events in the country is under way. Time is the enemy of the big-money calf roper; the hand on the stopwatch portends his financial fate. His success or failure is calibrated in fractions of a second. While a new star roper sometimes rises rapidly, an old-time rodeo fan can usually scan the names on a program and with a reasonable degree of accuracy predict the top few slots. A calf roper is an exotic mixture of superb athlete and competent technician. His horse is trained to near perfection and mirrors a mighty investment. His ropes are guarded; his uniform universal; his practice never-ending.

A few years ago, a stranger from New Mexico dragged his creaking horse trailer into the Prescott Fairgrounds a day before the rodeo was to start. The trailer could hardly deny its origin in backyard construction. What little stability it did have came from baling wire and high hopes. The horse it transported was a nice looking pony, but its quality was heavily camouflaged by the appearance of its rider. He was a young man in his twenties, with an undisciplined head of hair which had never seen a hat nor been recently caressed by a comb. His physique was hidden within the tunnels of a pair of blue denim bib overalls. The foundation of this rustic apparition was a pair of G.I. high-lace shoes. It was before the days of image making but, nevertheless, the stranger had done a superb job. The whole picture shouted "sucker" and echoed "soft touch." He entered the calf roping and out of three go-rounds, caught once with high time, failed to catch, and somehow won a third-place day money.

On the last afternoon of the rodeo, the word got around the roping chutes that the kid from New Mexico wanted to bet $500 on a three-calf average, matched roping. It was too tempting to ridicule, so the locals decided to make the pot really worthwhile. When the match was finally agreed on, somewhere between four and five thousand dollars was up for grabs. One of the smoothest man-and-horse machines ever to charge out of a roping chute was the kid's opponent. I am not a cruel man so I have blotted his name from my memory. He roped well, he roped very well indeed, as he always did. It was a symphony of man and horse and rope, liberally seasoned with coordination and attaining crescendos of timing and agility.

But it was not good enough. Three times the kid and his horse left the chute like a rocket, and three times the loop sped toward his calf like a well-aimed arrow. He left the saddle like a ballet dancer and his dash to the calf, his flanking and tying it, was a blur of bib overalls, brogan shoes, and blue denim. He was faultless. He left town a few minutes later with about five thousand dollars in his ample pockets. The natty local boys reflected and grumbled for several days; they allowed that "the kid was a good roper, but he needed polish." Perhaps he did, for he never came back.

The Gentleman General

In the West Point class of 1852 were forty-three cadets. George Crook, a farm boy from Ohio, was academically ranked thirty-eighth in that group. His French would barely permit the reading of a menu. His math was marginal and the little information he had gleaned regarding chemistry was a frail cog for his career.

In his four years at the academy he never left the ranks. But he was a humanist. He spoke of the philosophers, quoted the poets, and used his native tongue well and leanly. In the thirty-eight years of military life which followed his graduation, he rose to the rank of major general and while he was described as the greatest Indian fighter of all times, he was not. He was, however, a genius in Indian control and administration.

The innovation of the Army pack mule and the use of native scouts were some of his contributions. He learned to think like the Indian and came to understand him – attributes which sharpened his field effectiveness. General Crook spent his entire military career on the frontier with the exception of four years' Civil War service; on two separate occasions he conducted extensive Apache campaigns in the Territory of Arizona.

While he deplored the use of frontal military strength against the Indian, he used it moderately and skillfully when no alternative existed. His officers and men agreed that "in our hour of danger, Crook would be found on the skirmish line, not in the telegraph office." Both soldier and brave developed a profound respect for the quality of the man.

Thirty-two years after his graduation from West Point, General Crook returned to the banks of the Hudson to speak to the cadets. What he said in that obscure speech was, unhappily, never noted by the various bodies engaged in formulating policy for Indian affairs. One passage is especially easy to relate to contemporary Indian and human relations in general.

With all his faults, and he has many, the American Indian is not half so bad as he has been painted. He is cruel in war, treacherous at times, and not overly cleanly. But so were our forefathers. His nature, however, is responsive to a treatment which assures him that it is based upon justice, truth, honesty, and common sense; it is not impossible that with a fair and square system of dealing with him the American Indian would make a better citizen than many who neglect the duties and abuse the privileges of that proud title.

In those few words, George Crook, a farm boy from Ohio, the mediocre student, opened vistas which our national policy has yet to probe.

The Hopi Way

The first thing he saw when he opened his eyes that morning was a hazy gray veil of smoke floating from the ashes of last night's fire. The sun had just begun to penetrate the frail little cedars that formed the rocky bay where we were camped.

Here in the heart of the Hopi country he drew some water from the Igloo can into old coffee grounds, added some fresh ones, and placed the coffee pot on a greasy Coleman stove. He hated to get dressed.

For five years now, he had worked for the Hopi on their land claims. As a practicing anthropologist he had been able to do much for them to establish their claims and protect their tribal lands. But they had forced him into a new role; they trusted him, and at their request he had made the trip to Washington to argue their cause on policy in tribal administration. He had met with little success. His pleas on behalf of the Hopi had fallen on the unsympathetic ears of the Bureau of Indian Affairs.

Now this morning he must go to the pueblo of the Hopi priest and tell the old man of the unyielding attitude he had faced in Washington. After coffee and juice and a broken fried egg, he went to his tent to get a pair of old field boots as a gift for the old man. He put them in the four-wheeler and drove reluctantly into the village.

Gently he knocked on a shattered screen door. A pumpkin-shaped Hopi woman met him and nodded toward a chair at their table. The amenities were observed. A cigarette was offered, which the old Indian placed in the middle of his mouth and unhurriedly puffed, holding it with both his hands.

Unobtrusively, thick black coffee was poured into enamel cups and placed before the two men. The boots, together with a plastic bag of bird feathers, were handed to the old man. His ancient eyes gleamed their thanks.

Slowly and softly the anthropologist told the old Indian what his government had said. The Hopi must do this, they cannot do that, this has been decided, that must no longer be permitted. The old bronze face listened without a clue of emotion.

When the white man had finished his recital of rejection, the Indian sensed his sorrow. "Do not feel bad. You have done all you could do. Do not worry about it. It does not make any difference, for we are not going to do it anyway."

As he drove away the professor smiled.

"The old man's people have survived for centuries on this brittle mesa."

"Washington is a long, long way from Oraibi."

"They are Hopi and the Hopi Road is long, strong, and endless."

He headed back to a happy camp.

Incident in Bisbee

A few minutes after seven on the evening of December 10, 1883, six men rode out of the desert of Cochise County and into the town of Bisbee. Five of the men swung down from their horses and handed their bridle reins to the sixth man. They entered the Goldwater Store, which was managed by a Mr. Castañeda, and demanded the contents of the safe, using their leveled guns to urge obedience and dispatch. Two thousand dollars was removed from the safe, and a canvas sack containing an additional one thousand dollars was plucked from beneath the pillow of Mr. Castañeda's bed in the rear of the store. When the bandits left the building, they opened fire on some surprised citizens of Bisbee who happened to be passing by. Five innocent men were shot down in the streets. This was the Bisbee Massacre.

In less than a month, James Howard, O.W. Sample, Dan Dowd, William Delaney, Dan Kelley, and the man who held their horses, John Heith, were placed in the Tombstone jail.

In February, 1884, following the trial, Judge Pinney sentenced all five men to be hung in the Tombstone Jail yard on March 28th. The horse holder, twenty-eight-year old John Heith was sentenced to life in the Territorial Prison at Yuma. The citizens of Bisbee were not satisfied.

On the morning of February 22, 1884, promptly at 8:00 a.m., the Tombstone jailer, Bill Ward, answered a knock on the jail door, thinking it was the Chinese cook delivering his breakfast. Seven Bisbee men, armed and unmasked, quickly took John Heith from his cell and placed a new rope (purchased at Goldwaters, "The Best Always") around his neck. A half block from the courthouse, one of the Bisbee men climbed a pole and passed the rope over the crossbar of a newly erected telegraph pole. The condemned man made but one request: "Boys, please don't fill my body with bullets when I am dead." The request was honored. A placard was placed on the pole which read as follows:

John Heith was hanged to this pole by the citizens of Cochise County for participation in the Bisbee Massacre as proven accessory at 8:20 a.m. February 22, 1884. Washington's Birthday. Advance Arizona!

The five remaining participants were legally hanged in the Tombstone Jail yard on March 28, 1884 at 1:15 p.m.

Dead were:

> Five Bisbee Citizens
> Five Arizona desperadoes
> One young Texan

The Bisbee Massacre had passed into Arizona History.

Territorial Medicare

In the latter part of March, 1889, a young Denver photographer agreed to assume an exciting job. Franklin A. Nims was a thirty-year-old bachelor and a native of Kansas, skilled in photography.

Denver businessman and real-estate promoter Frank M. Brown had organized the Denver, Colorado Canyon and Pacific Railroad in an attempt to bring to reality an incredible dream of a prospector. The prospector, S.S. Harper, after observing a number of railroad surveys in northern Arizona, visualized a railroad which would follow the water-level route on the Colorado River from the west slope of the Rocky Mountains to the Gulf of California, then turn north along the Coast and terminate in San Diego.

An engineering survey to determine the feasibility of such a route was the first order of business; this was to be done by a party of seventeen men in boats surveying the entire river route from Green River, Utah, to the mouth of the Colorado River. The responsibility of such an awesome engineering feat rested on the capable shoulders of Robert Brewster Stanton, an able civil engineer, hired by the president of the Denver, Colorado Canyon and Pacific Railroad, Frank M. Brown. Nims was offered the job of photographing the canyons which the route would traverse, thus furnishing evidence to skeptical Eastern investors.

The party left Green River, Utah, on May 25, 1889, in six shallow-draft, brittle cedar boats, aimed unerringly toward disaster. Hurried preparations and scanty supplies assured tragedy. Businessman Brown regarded life preservers as extravagant, if not a cowardly, expenditure. Forty-six days later, Frank Brown drowned, disappearing into a whirlpool in Marble Canyon; five days following his death, the river gulped down two more members of the group into the throat of eternity. The remaining fourteen disheartened men climbed the cliffs and retreated to Denver.

For the next four months, the future of the Denver, Colorado Canyon and Pacific Railroad was reassessed. In Waukegan, Illinois, three boats were built to rigid specifications. New equipment was purchased and financial reorganization arranged.

On December 10, 1889, the new boats of the second Stanton survey took to the river at Crescent Creek in Glen Canyon. Twelve men made up this party, among them the wiry and adventuresome Franklin A. Nims. He seemed to love his photographic work and constantly roamed the ridges of the river bed looking for better pictorial composition.

Christmas dinner was a festive affair at Lee's Ferry. A Mormon family by the name of Johnson operated the ferry at this time and hospitality being a tenet of their faith, they contributed generously to the holiday table.

In his diary, Nims mentioned departing from Lee's Ferry on December 28, to again enter Marble Canyon, where the party had previously met disaster. January 1, 1890, was a date for Franklin Nims to remember, for on this day, seeking a shelf on which to take a panoramic view of the river, he fell twenty-two feet to the rocks below. Hurtling downward, his body obscured from the view of his companions, they heard only his groan of submission to unconsciousness. Several moments passed before members of the group located him.

The broken body of Franklin Nims lay on the rocky floor of Marble Canyon. It was obvious that at least one leg was fractured just above the ankle. Blood oozed from his mouth and ears, strongly supporting the suspicion of internal injury. He was unconscious and mercifully unaware of the problem his condition presented to the second Stanton survey. The closest settlement where care and comfort might be available was Lee's Ferry. Getting there meant climbing 1,700 feet of canyon wall of various dimension and grade. Once this was done, 35 miles of winter desert had to be crossed on foot to obtain help.

First, a cot was made from two oak oars with cross pieces of driftwood and canvas for a cover. After splinting his fractured leg with an old rubber boot, his companions placed Nims on the cot and secured him firmly to it. He was then loaded into one of the boats and taken ten miles down the river where a likely escape route was located up a side canyon.

Early on the morning of January 3, two full days after the accident, Mr. Stanton, together with John Hislop and Harry McDonald, key members of the survey party, left the camp where Nims still lay unconscious. The three men began the climb to the rim of the side canyon. At noon they reached the top. Engineer Stanton started his long, footsore trek to Lee's Ferry in hopes of getting a wagon to transport the patient. McDonald and Hislop returned to the river camp to organize a team to carry Nims on his stretcher up the 1,700-foot cliff the next morning.

Hislop and McDonald selected six men to help them transport Nims up the canyon wall. Four men carried the improvised stretcher, while the other four carried food and extra blankets; frequently the teams switched off.

The lower portion of the side canyon contained many boulders which at some undetermined time had separated from the cliffs above and thundered down the side. The rescue team carried their burden over, around, and sometimes even under these ectopic rock masses which were wedged into the narrow walls. One rocky bench after another challenged the climbers. At times, the slopes on which they rested were so steep, rocks had to be placed on the frame of the stretcher to prevent it from sliding into space. In the first three miles, they climbed 700 feet; the 1,000 feet that remained became progressively steeper, the loose talus benches sometimes sloping as much as 45 degrees. After hours of heroic struggle, Nim's stretcher was rigged with rope and raised slowly up the final 30 feet of sheer rock wall. They had reached the rim.

The following morning, Robert Stanton, with his Mormon friend Mr. Johnson, arrived by wagon from Lee's Ferry. Nims was placed on a mattress in the rear of the wagon and taken to Johnson's home. Twelve days after he had fallen, Nims opened his dim eyes to consciousness at Lee's Ferry. He stayed with the Johnson family for four days, trying to gain strength. On January 16, a Mormon mother and her two sons placed him in their wagon and headed for the railroad at Winslow; nine days later they arrived.

At Winslow he received medical attention and managed to get a check cashed by a local merchant who was, as Nims was, an ardent member of the Odd Fellows Lodge. The Winslow Odd Fellows made arrangements for his railroad passage to his home in Denver. A month from the day he had fallen in Marble Canyon, Nims entered the hospital in Denver.

On March 17, 1890, the Stanton survey emerged from the Grand Canyon into the open country and a placid Colorado River. On the same day in Denver, Franklin A. Nims also emerged from the plaster casts which had encased his legs. However, he had other problems. The Denver, Colorado Canyon and Pacific Railroad carried no accident insurance and to compound this oversight, the benevolent rail company had struck him from the payroll on the day he fell from the cliff.

Growing Pains

The year 1917 was an unusual one in the history of Arizona. On November 7, 1917, Thomas E. Campbell, Republican candidate for the office of governor, was declared to have defeated the incumbent, George W.P. Hunt, by 30 votes. Governor Hunt contested the election vehemently and on January 1, 1918, both Thomas E. Campbell and George W.P. Hunt were sworn in as Governor of Arizona in their own separate ceremonies.

Governor Hunt (if he could be called that) actually refused to vacate the Governor's Office in the Capitol Building, and Governor (?) Campbell opened his office in his own home, using a substantial zinc-topped kitchen table for a desk. The state treasurer, a Democrat, announced that he would not honor state checks signed by Campbell. The state auditor, also a Democrat, allowed as how he, too, would not allow the claims approved by Campbell. Shortly after these startling announcements, the state fiscal officers were advised by the court that they had better apply the same policy to George W.P. Hunt's signature on state checks.

The Legislature convened in routine session, and both men mounted the podium to address the legislators. The State of Arizona was five years old and the United States was about to become involved in World War I. All things considered, Arizona's new year was not off to the finest possible start.

There were other little signs of dissent and disaster also occurring in January, 1918. The Arizona Press Club was formally organized; this undoubtedly caused politicians to shudder. Open revolt occurred in the Arizona National Guard on the Mexican border at Naco and Company M held a protest march on the parade ground demanding they be sent home ("Hell no, I won't go," some fifty years early).

Now the Great White Father spoke from his Washington throne, and United States postal authorities ruled that all official mail for the Governor of Arizona be delivered to Secretary of State Sidney P. Osborn, until the courts decided the issue of who was Governor of Arizona.

The Legislature, ignoring the gubernatorial problem, fought hammer and tong in a bitter battle over the design of the state flag. Many members thought it too closely resembled the rising sun banner of Japan. (This complaint was voiced again in World War II.) The flag design was finally adopted as it appears today. In the midst of this chaos, the Sheriff of Pima County saw fit to pour twenty thousand dollars worth of contraband liquor out on the courthouse lawn. (A clear case of police brutality.) As if this wasn't enough, the Attorney General ruled that Arizona's dry law was valid and before the Third Legislature adjourned on March 9 of that year, it passed anti-gambling and red-light abatement bills, creating an even more somber environment in the newest state in the Union.

On May 22, 1918, Superior Court Judge R.C. Stanford ruled that the examination of all ballots showed that Thomas E. Campbell had defeated George W.P. Hunt by thirty to fifty votes for the office of Governor of Arizona.

In the meantime, down at the border, the City of Nogales asked for state aid, for their jail was overflowing with draft dodgers from all over the country who were taken into custody in the border city.

While Governor Campbell was giving this matter his attention, attorneys for ex-Governor Hunt established rules for a rehearing of the election contest before the Supreme Court. Then on December 22, the Supreme Court reversed the decision of the Superior Court and declared that George W.P. Hunt was legally Governor of Arizona, although Thomas E. Campbell had served in this capacity for eleven months and three weeks.

The Copper Queen Consolidated Mining Company, apparently so embarrassed by all these shenanigans, changed its name to the Phelps Dodge Corporation. Many old-timers predicted the new name would never catch on.

On Christmas morning, 1918, Thomas E. Campbell turned the Governor's office back to George W.P. Hunt. The press reported that as he did so, he quoted from Dickens' Christmas Carol. (Probably, "Bah! Humbug!") The traumatic year of 1918 in Arizona came to a close.

Prescott Frontier Days Rodeo, 1928. Left to right, Pat McIlvain, Budge Ruffner, Bob Boy Barrett and Joe McIlvain. Photograph courtesy of the Joe McIlvain Collection.

Always Go by the Book

In the spring of 1867, an extensive surveying expedition was organized by the Kansas Pacific Railroad Company to determine a feasible route through Kansas, Colorado, New Mexico, and Arizona to the southern portion of California. Two previous surveys had been made in the same general area by the young Army officers Edward F. Beale and Amiel W. Whipple. This new probe, however, was headed by the illustrious General W.J. Palmer and was to study the character of the country in minute detail; therefore, it was financed much more handsomely than the previous two.

Joining this group at the last minute as a photographer (in name only), was a young English geologist, Dr. William A. Bell. He later published in London the book *New Tracks in North America,* portions of which were written by several of his traveling companions. Two possible routes across Arizona were investigated by this group, one in southern Arizona and northern Mexico (the Gila Route), and one across the northern portion of the state (the 35th parallel), now in use today. Bell chose to travel the southern route while General Palmer scouted the northern area with a small group of soldiers and Army mules. The line the Santa Fe Railroad now uses from the Little Colorado River west, past San Francisco Peaks, towards the Colorado River at Needles was thought by Palmer to be too high and arid. He proved right on both counts.

In late November, 1867, General Palmer left his camp located in the high country somewhere south of the present

Flagstaff and headed southwest, seeking a lower route west for the proposed railroad. His description of Val de Chino (Chino Valley) was most prophetic: "A splendid meadow ten miles in width, lying between the Aztec Range and the Black Mountains. It is covered with the finest grama grass which gives the name to the valley. The average elevation of this great valley is about 4,500 feet above tide. The soil is rich and needs only water to enable the breadstuffs of an entire state to be raised there."

Still seeking a feasible route, Palmer's small band headed down-river from the headquarters of the Verde to return to their camp in the mountains. As the Verde River canyon grew progressively deeper they climbed out its north bank and struck out in a northeasterly direction. They soon came to "a most precipitous canyon filled with ruins of an ancient culture and sprinkled with huge boulders." Here they made a grave tactical error. Entering Sycamore Canyon, "rather than climb the east side which deemed too difficult, we headed north along the floor of the deep ravine." The General admits his mistake, a prime rule of warfare: "Cross a canyon direct, or go around it, but never use the floor of a canyon for a travel route in hostile country."

Barely thirty minutes had passed before it happened. With a chorus of war whoops, Apaches opened a slow, single-shot, and fortunately, inaccurate fire which peppered the General's small scouting detail. Palmer was candid in describing the pall of panic which descended on his men. But, being imbued with the discipline of the profession, he ordered five men to scatter their mules and to scale the west side of Sycamore on foot, armed with their repeating rifles. Using bows to reinforce their ancient firearms, the Indians scattered to naturally camouflaged positions. Arrows whined through the undergrowth as the General ordered another small group to dig in behind the large boulders to cover the ascent of the soldiers on the west wall. A third group was soon ordered to scale the east side of the rocky gorge. These men Palmer led, after ordering the remaining muleteers to escape with the animals down the canyon toward the Verde River. Some forty-eight hours later the detail regrouped, exhausted and hungry.

93

It was not a victory, only a well designed escape that owed its success to superior fire power and field innovation. On December 8, 1967, General W.J. Palmer, while resting in camp, recorded the event in the clipped and clinical vernacular of his profession.

Budge with son, George, at Sharlot Hall Museum in 1954. Budge's parents were friends of Miss Sharlot Hall, first woman to hold office in the Arizona Territory and founder of the Governor's Mansion Museum, later renamed after Sharlot's death in 1943. Budge was a Boy Scout when Miss Hall established the museum and helped collect pennies to defray the cost of removing the remains of early military scout, Pauline Weaver, from the Presido in San Francisco and reburying them on the grounds of the museum. Photograph courtesy of the Ruffner Collection.

The Steak House

An old friend, Gail Wingfield, related an incident when he was in a philosophical mood discussing the various kinds of crises he has to meet when dealing with the public.

Gail for years operated the Mormon Lake Steak House, a well-regarded beef and beverage bistro a few miles south of Flagstaff on the shores of once wet Mormon Lake. Gail served steaks there, cooked over oak coals. They were slightly smaller in size than the state of Rhode Island and a good deal more flavorful. In addition to this worthy endeavor, he presided over a well-stocked bar which served as the soul of the rambling building.

The days were quiet there with just an occasional traveler dropping in, but when the sun slid over the west rim of Oak Creek Canyon, the thirsty, hungry, and misunderstood merged at this mecca to wage a ruthless war against starvation, dehydration, and loneliness.

Late one afternoon, Gail was going about the routine chores in preparation for the evening onslaught. The telephone rang. Gail picked up the inconsiderate instrument and mumbled a hurried hello. A concerned voice at the other end inquired:

"Is this the Mormon Lake Steak House?"

"That's right," said Gail.

"Are you the Bishop?" was the next question the caller directed.

"If there's a Bishop around here I guess I'm it," responded Gail.

A quizzical pause followed, then finally the conversation resumed.

"I am calling for Brother so-and-so," the caller continued. "He is sick and not doing at all well. There is some question as to his recovery. Could you come to see him tonight? I am sure your visit would be helpful."

Gail was puzzled.

"I would like to," he volunteered, "but I am just getting the fires started and the bar set up for the night. It's kind of a bad time for me."

A stunned silence. Then again:

"Are you sure this is the Mormon Lake Stake House?"

Gail seemed annoyed.

"Sure I'm sure. We've been here for years and do a hell of a business."

"Oh!" said the caller, "you spell it S-T-E-A-K. I was calling the S-T-A-K-E house."

There the confusion ended. Both telephones clicked back onto their cradles.

Politics Is Politics

Phoenix was new. On October 20, 1869, a citizen's committee, which called itself the Salt River Town Association, had met and selected an area one and a half miles long and one mile wide, and agreed that this mesquite flat would be named Phoenix. The bird was arising from her nest of ashes. There were a few appointed county officials, but the first election was not scheduled until May of 1871. There was no jail, but only two arrests had been made the previous six months, and these were for minor offenses traced to undisciplined sociability. The Goldwater brothers had agreed to sell their large, barn-like store on Washington Street to the county for $3,000, and this became the courthouse – complete with jail, judge's chambers, and the basic offices of county government.

At this point, only one man had declared himself a candidate for sheriff of Maricopa County; Thomas Barnum, a member of the "Salt River Town Association": a quiet, chronically ill-at-ease type who would rather belly up to a chess board than a bar. He was known throughout the Valley as a shrewd dealer. By Christmas, two more candidates announced their intentions of becoming Maricopa County's first elected sheriff – "Whispering Jim" Favorite, a local loudmouth who happened to be blessed with a name fraught with political potential, and J.N. Chenoweth, one of the first disappointed miners to move to Phoenix from the surrounding mountains. Soon stories began to be repeated in such chambers of slander as saloons, barber shops, and livery stables. Chenoweth said this about Favorite. Favorite said that about Chenoweth. Oddly enough, the name of the establishment member, Thomas Barnum, was never mentioned. Violent quotes, however, concerning Favorite and Chenoweth continued to be repeated and magnified at the local watering holes.

Soon the indifference which had existed between Chenoweth and Favorite fermented into hostility. Barnum stood on the sidelines and watched the cauldron of ill will approach its boiling point. He did nothing to stop it, and there was some evidence that he enthusiastically fed the flames. Soon the black bud of hate burst into full bloom – when Chenoweth and Favorite met face to face and one of Phoenix's first murders was committed. Chenoweth gunned down Whispering Jim Favorite. A promising Arizona political career came to an end on a dusty desert lot. Chenoweth was tried for the murder but was acquitted and advised to leave the Territory. He readily accepted the suggestion.

In the May election, Thomas Barnum was unopposed for the office of sheriff. It wasn't exactly a Shirley Temple campaign technique, but it nevertheless served to elect the first sheriff of Maricopa County.

A Crowd Pleaser

In the southern section of Coconino County, a few miles east of the Black Canyon freeway, is a small circular body of water known as Stoneman Lake, named after General George Stoneman, one of the most controversial Army commanders to serve in the Military District of Arizona.

Stoneman was not a renowned diplomat. He was blunt, tactless, abrasive, and domineering. Aloof and pigheaded, he seldom failed to offend subordinates and superiors alike. If he had any decent personality traits, perhaps it could be said he was impartial in his obnoxiousness. He passed through southern Arizona in 1846 as a young lieutenant attached to the Mormon Battalion during the Mexican War. He returned to Arizona in 1870 as Commander of the Military Department of Arizona and Southern California with headquarters at Fort Whipple.

Stoneman was literally "in the saddle" of this command, although his Arizona career lasted only eleven months. In this brief time he was criticized bitterly within the territory for his "soft" policy toward the Indians. In the East, equal criticism was leveled against him by politicians and do-gooders of the Indian Ring, a group of people who were convinced the Indian could be subdued without the use of violence. They complained loudly of his killing the hostile and so-called friendly Apache alike.

In Arizona, Stoneman's policy of furnishing supplies, seed, and farm implements to nomadic bands of Apaches infuriated the citizens of the Territory. The pampering of a

99

proven enemy was even then an unpopular foreign policy. Anyone who has attempted farming in Arizona, however, must agree with Stoneman, than the raising of crops in this area would consume more time and ingenuity than the raising of scalps.

After completing the building of the military road from Horsehead Crossing on the Little Colorado River to Fort Apache, early in 1871, Stoneman was relieved of his command. He was later elected governor of California and served in that capacity until 1887.

Death silenced the forked tongue of the old general in New York City in 1894. The huge church where his funeral was held was crowded with hundreds of people attending the service. Following the rites, a small group of his old troopers stood on the steps outside discussing the phenomenon. They remarked how strange it was that a man who had made so few military, political, and personal friends should have such a large crowd present at his funeral. A major asked an old top sergeant of the general's if he could explain it.

"Certainly, sir," the old trooper remarked, "it just goes to prove, give the people what they want and they will turn out."

All Hell Needs Is Water

He came here from Albuquerque in 1928 and went to work for the Bank of Arizona. He was a dapper, warm, and witty man whose eyes smiled with his lips – a specialist in livestock banking. People liked him, for he had the gift of honest interest, whether his conversation was with a shoeshine boy, or a mining company president. He spoke a little New Mexico Spanish and dressed Madison Avenue. He was his own man.

There was, of course, dire need for livestock loans in Arizona. Most ranches were established family operations with depression at the door and drought crossing the fence line. In spite of what the movies told us every Saturday afternoon, the fact was that the local friendly bank saved more ranches than Tom Mix, Hoot Gibson, and the Seventh Cavalry ever saw.

When a loan request was received by the bank, he would get in his car and drive to the ranch to learn first hand its problems and potential. He was a competent and knowledgeable observer. The local ranchers knew the futility of trying to secure their loans with calf tallies and cow tracks; he knew an honest count and was familiar with the first subtle evidence of overgrazing.

One of the good customers of the bank was a pioneer Mexican-American family, whose ancestors drove their cattle overland from California in territorial times. The banker was visiting their ranch to aid in the requested loan and seemed favorably impressed with their management and industry. As he walked to his car for the trip back to town, he said: "Mr. Chávez, you have a good, well-run ranch here; all you really need is a little more dependable water supply." The old vaquero smiled. "Mr. White," he said, "all hell needs is water."

Budge and son, George, on the Mogollon Rim in 1958. Photograph courtesy of the Ruffner Collection.

Years Ago

I ran across a dirty book the other day. It was jammed behind a stack of old magazines stored on a shelf. The dust on it must have been an inch thick. It was the 1870 Federal Census for Prescott, Arizona Territory. It proudly stated that at the time this census was taken, the town of Prescott had 151 dwellings, 45 families, 564 males, 111 females. It proclaimed that there were no blind members of the community but there was one citizen generally regarded as insane. (In many ways we haven't made a hell of a lot of progress.)

Those interviewed by the census taker were asked to give their names (a great many of them had several), age (I didn't find anyone over 69 and the youngest one was little Laura Dickson, age three months), sex (in those days you could tell the difference), occupation, value of property and place of birth.

Bradley C. Bain said he was 60 years old, a gambler, born in New Hampshire. Mary Anschultz was a milliner, age 18, but had no idea where she was born. Joseph Baker, age 34, came to Prescott from his native Ohio and told the census taker he was a speculator; that classification gave him a wide operating base. George Washington Barnard was the postmaster. He claimed he was 36 years old, born in Michigan and was worth two thousand and fifty dollars. You won't find many postmasters who have done that well nowadays. Phillip Allen was a 20-year old seaman. Even when Granite Creek ran brim to brim, that one must have driven the boys at the employment office up the wall. Joseph Callagan, born in Ireland, was a tailor; John Callahan, born in Ireland, was a blacksmith. Having seen some products of Irish tailors, my bet is that they both went to the same blacksmith school. The richest man in the census was a Scot named John Goulder Campbell. He had property worth $42,000 and was married to a swinging wife named Carmelita who was born in Chile.

There was a character by the name of Willard Rice who was a scout and wagon master. A family by the name of Rice lives in Prescott today; they have three station wagons cramming their carport, but with five kids, what else can you do? Theodore Putz was a cigar maker from Austria and John Laughlin a cordwainer (if you find out what that is, let me know).*

John M. Roundtree was a 38-year-old lawyer, with a wife and three little girls. Forty-one year old John Langford Taylor from Kentucky was the sheriff and Sam Smith, 22, was a miner from Maine. Also listed was Thomas Hall, a circus actor from New York, two school teachers and 27 barkeepers, which may give you some idea what the priorities were. Henry Waring Fleury was the Probate Judge. We have a street named after him.

Calvin Jackson was a cooper from Illinois, A. Hin from China, a laundryman. Butchers, cooks brewers, saddlemakers, wheelwrights, printers, artists, watch makers, stone carvers and carpenters all were a part of Prescott a hundred and one years ago. Dr. James Nuten McCandless, at age 32, was a practicing physician-surgeon. Two young ladies, Maggie Taylor of California and Jennie McKennie of New York, both listed their occupations as "fancy woman." They did, however, refuse to disclose their assets.

*Editors' Note: According to Random House Dictionary of the English Language, a cordwainer is 1.) one who makes shoes from cordovan leather, 2.) a shoemaker; cobbler.

It's Possible

On March 3, 1855, the 33rd Congress of the United States passed a bill appropriating $30,000.00 for the War Department to purchase camels and dromedaries to aid in conquering the great American desert. Jefferson Davis was at the time Secretary of War and later became President of the Confederacy. Secretary Davis assigned Major Henry C. Wayne of the U.S. Army, and Lt. D.D. Porter of the U.S. Navy the unique duty of visiting the Middle East and purchasing these odd beasts, primarily in Egypt and Syria. After two trips to North Africa, the U.S.S. Supply had by February 17, 1857, landed 103 camels and five Arab "camel jockeys" in Texas, near Galveston. In the fall of 1857 Lt. Edward F. Beale of the U.S. Topographical Engineers was ordered to open a major road from Ft. Defiance near the present Arizona, New Mexico border, to the eastern frontier of California. This route later became the main Santa Fe railroad route across northern Arizona. This project proved to be the acid test for the camels. They carried six to eight hundred pounds each at a remarkable rate of speed across the rugged terrain. The abrasive granite and volcanic malapai which were so damaging to the hooves of horse and mules had little effect on the tough feet of the camels. They grazed eagerly on the native browse, dried grasses and stunted desert shrubs. The infrequency of water holes seemed to have little effect on their efficiency. But the camels did have their shortcomings. Their contempt for their American handlers was frequently manifested with a bite in the back. This unfortunate characteristic did little to endear the camels to the men in the survey group. One mule-skinner described them as ornery, obstinate, stubborn, and completely incorrigible. And this doesn't even get down to some really basic mule-skinner terminology. It was also a fact that these strange beasts terrified other domestic animals. Horses and mules panicked on sight; this, of course, caused great problems. The army packers knew nothing about packing camels so they were frequently sore-backed and surly. They grew increasingly difficult to handle, and finally the skinners complained of their peculiar and potent body odor. While the Beale survey using the camels was a complete success, the prejudicial attitude of the men towards the capabilities of the camels, and the approaching Civil War brought the experiment to a hasty conclusion. Some of the strange one and two humped animals escaped to roam the desert and others were released by the Army on purpose. Some were sold to zoos, circuses and ranches for $31.00 a head. Bethel Coapwood, who was later to become a Confederate colonel, purchased fourteen and sent them to Mexico where he planned to retire. For the next eighty years reports of sightings of wild camels in the deserts of Nevada, Arizona, California and New Mexico periodically appeared. The last account of a camel being seen came forth in 1939 after a 37 year moratorium on camel sighting. It was reported by a miner who was returning from a party held in the desert a few miles west of Ajo, Arizona. Company picnics held in the hospitable desert, and breaking the mundane routine of an isolated mining town can easily become overly festive. A fuschia-hued elephant could fit snugly into the credibility gap, or a flying saucer, but a camel? Never!

Tucson?

It was a windy day in Tucson and the aggressive desert breeze filled the air with a fine, chalky dust. A rough lumber platform had been erected to serve as a stand for the ceremonies, and the speaker for the occasion, the distinguished William S. Oury, was adequate but thoughtfully brief. In a matter of minutes, the arrival of the railroad in Tucson had been publicly observed. The dedication was over, the crowd began to trickle back to the corners of commerce in the Old Pueblo. Many of the men in attendance were subconsciously disappointed by the lack of magnitude of the event and a number of them entered a nearby saloon to personally extend the festivities.

The saloon session was a creative appendix and each ounce of whiskey consumed, seemed to generate a new idea to add a belated promotional flair to the arrival of the railroad in the city. It was the expansive Charles D. Poston, "The Father of Arizona" who suggested the telegrams. He urged they be sent to the President of the United States, the Vice President, Speaker of the House and the Mayors of such sizeable cities as New York, Chicago, Philadelphia and San Francisco, announcing the arrival of the railroad in the Old Pueblo. When this was done, the question was raised - had anyone of genuine prominence been overlooked? As more and more drinks were poured, an Irish railroad worker urged that certainly His Holiness, the Pope, should be extended this same recognition. This was eagerly agreed upon, and the telegram read as follows:

107

"Tucson, A.T., March 25, 1880.
To His Holiness, Pope Leo XIII:
We beg to inform your Excellency that Tucson,
founded three hundred years ago by members of
your faith, has this day been linked to the outside
world by rails of steel.
　　　　　Signed: The Citizens of Tucson."

In 1880, the telegraph messages out of Tucson were relayed via Phoenix, Yuma and San Diego. The quantity of telegrams outgoing from the Tucson saloon that March afternoon was apparently noticed by the various relay operators along the line. Toward evening, the acknowledgements began to be delivered to the celebrants. Congratulations from the President of the United States and the mayors of important cities were read, accompanied by the cheers of the multitude. To this day, citizens of Tucson blame what happened next on the Phoenix telegrapher. Tears glistened in the corners of Irish eyes as the message from Rome was read:

"Citizens of Tucson:
His Holiness, the Pope, congratulates Tucson,
founded more than three hundred years ago by
members of His faith, on the arrival of the
railroad to your city. Incidentally, where the
Hell is Tucson:
　　　　　Signed: Leo XIII"

A century has hardly begun to erase that cruel remark, seared on the soul of a city.

What Arizona Means to Me

What Arizona means to me?
Perhaps just a Palo Verde tree;
A star filled night, a sun-warmed day,
A dusty Indian child at play.
A desert bloom, a snow-capped peak,
Roaring river, dry stone creek.
The brittle ground of ancient battle,
Ten thousand head of white-faced cattle.
An arrow point beneath the dirt,
A rusty spur and rawhide quirt.
A mine shaft dug into a slope
Which once held promises and hope.
Now we speed on past these things
Or look below from metal wings.
I come from this, yet cannot see
What Arizona means to me.

- Budge Ruffner

THE NEVADAN

The reader will smile, chuckle and laugh aloud while thoroughly enjoying the collection of cleverly written vignettes of frontier life in the West by Lester Ward "Budge" Ruffner, an author with deep roots of his own in Arizona history...This small book is packed full of episodes...most of the stories belong to Arizona although a few are of general western appeal.

- January 23, 1973
(Las Vegas Review Journal)

OFFICE OF THE GOVERNOR
STATE HOUSE
JACK WILLIAMS
GOVERNOR

PHOENIX, ARIZONA 85007

December 8, 1972

Dear Budge,

...I did grab a few moments now and then to peruse your book, <u>All Hell Needs is Water</u>. Budge, it is a thoroughly professional and remarkably delightful book.

...You are indeed to be commended for a very delightful and warmly human series of tales from early Arizona.

Warmest personal regards,

Jack Williams

The Sidney Herald

This newly-published panorama of Western Americana serves up lesser known nuggets of the lusty history of the Southwest in a series of fascinating vignettes . . . even an evaluation of the rainfall of the region, or lack of it, as summed up by one *vaquero* who observed "all hell needs is water."

- January 31, 1973
(Sidney, Montana)

VALLEY NATIONAL BANK

RICHARD H. BISHOPP
MANAGER

COOLIDGE, ARIZONA

January 15, 197e

Dear Budge,

....I received a copy of your book, <u>All Hell Needs is Water</u>....I read the book last night and could not put it down until I finished it. Several of the stories I really related to since I knew the participants. The one called "The Ringer" almost caused me to fall out of my chair because I was there the day that happened at the Prescott Rodeo and I have related that incident many times since...

Well, it certainly was a pleasure reading your book and I think it was great.

Best regards,

Richard H. Bishopp

All Hell Needs Is Water was selected to be part of the United States Information Agency's World of Paperbacks: American Bicentennial Book Exhibit which traveled in thirty-four foreign countries and was displayed in cities throughout Europe, Africa, the Near and Far East, South America and the U.S.S.R.